Courageous Women Rebels

The Women's Hall of Fame Series

COURAGEOUS WOMEN REBELS

JOY CRYSDALE

Second Story Press

Library and Archives Canada Cataloguing in Publication

Crysdale, Joy, 1952-
Courageous women rebels / Joy Crysdale.

(The women's hall of fame series)
Issued also in an electronic format.
ISBN 978-1-926920-99-3

1. Women social reformer—Biography—Juvenile literature.
2. Women political activists—Biography—Juvenile literature.
I. Title. II. Series: Women's hall of fame series

HN17.5.C79 2013   j303.48'409252   C2012-908179-5X

Editor: Kathryn White
Designer: Melissa Kaita
Cover photos and icons © istockphoto.com

Printed and bound in Canada

*Second Story Press gratefully acknowledges the support of the
Ontario Arts Council and the Canada Council for the Arts for our
publishing program. We acknowledge the financial support of the
Government of Canada through the Canada Book Fund.*

Published by
Second Story Press
20 Maud Street, Suite 401
Toronto, ON
M5V 2M5
www.secondstorypress.ca

*Dedicated to the courage and rebel spirits of my cousin,
Lois Kennedy, and my sister, Mary "Sue" Poirier.
They did not realize how much they would be missed.*

CONTENTS

INTRODUCTION

We love rebels – at least the ones in books and movies. They break the rules, turn a blind eye to authority, follow their own path, and don't care what anyone thinks. They are romantic figures, and we imagine we could be like them. In real life, though, most of us trudge along, doing what we're told, accepting the way things are. And we find real rebels a bit annoying.

Almost all the women in this book are a particular type of rebel. They are activists: people who devote themselves to change. They had the ability to see long before others did that slavery, inequality of women, inequality due to race, discrimination against people considered "different," cruelty to animals, political tyranny, and more, were terribly wrong. Then they tried to do something about it. Most people didn't understand what these women were rebelling against. They thought all these things were normal, the way it was supposed to be. And they wanted them to shut up.

None of the women in this book were willing to do that. Some of them lost their lives because of it. All of them put themselves at risk. They did so – and this is the most important point – not for their own sake, but because they saw there was something bigger and more important than their individual lives: a need for justice.

Olympe de Gouges of France was a visionary in the 1700s who called for the kind of women's rights that wouldn't be taken seriously until two centuries later. She was executed, and dismissed as insane. Former slave Sojourner Truth fought for the abolition of slavery and the vote for women in the 1800s. She would live to see one, but not the other, achieved.

Others also died before their goals were accomplished. Ruth First was killed by a letter bomb sent by South African police, before the racist system she worked to overthrow was finally dismantled. Sarojini Naidu lived to see the end of British rule in India, a cause she was jailed for numerous times. But she also campaigned for equality between men and women, and between all castes and religions in her country, and those battles remain to be won.

For more than forty years, Gloria Steinem has been a second-wave feminist leader. Although some of the movement's goals have been achieved, there have also been disheartening setbacks. Pacifist Joan Baez was able to see an end to the war in Vietnam, but there is never an end to war.

All the women in the book have remarkable personal stories and childhoods, but two that stand out are Leilani Muir and Temple Grandin. Leilani's mother put her in a mental institution, although there was nothing wrong with her. She was sterilized there – made physically incapable of having children – because the government believed so-called mental "defectives" were a threat to society. Temple's mother, on the other hand, never gave up on her autistic child. She saw her daughter earn her PhD and discover that autism could be a gift. Temple's autism allowed her to understand animals, whose rights she now fights for.

Michelle Douglas took on the biggest fight of her life with the support of her family. An outstanding officer, she was kicked out of the military because she was a lesbian. Shannen Koostachin's family taught her pride in her aboriginal heritage. That gave her the strength to organize, at age thirteen, what has been called the largest youth-led children's rights campaign in Canadian history.

These ten women had a variety of ways to get their messages out, from writing to music, from public speaking to the Internet, from journalism to the court system. Most believed in using non-violent methods, except for Ruth First, who became convinced peaceful means could not achieve her goal. Some were driven to do what they did because of religious faith, and many fought for women's rights in addition to their other goals. Seeking justice for others, they realized their own gender was not receiving equal rights.

There were so many women and causes that could have been included in *Courageous Women Rebels*. There simply wasn't room. However, to read more about environmentalists and other peace, native rights, and political activists, I refer readers to the other Women's Hall of Fame books.

It sometimes takes years, even centuries, to catch up to rebels whose clarity of thinking and daring action sets them apart. They are shining examples of how people can make a difference. Still, for those of us less-daring non-rebels, every day it is possible to see ways in which we can put others before ourselves, and make the bigger picture more important than the small things in our individual lives. It's not easy. It's incredibly hard. But I hope these women's stories inspire all of us to try.

Joy Crysdale

OLYMPE DE GOUGES

"Woman is born free and remains equal to man in rights."

1748 – 1793

Moments before she was to be executed in a Paris city square, Olympe de Gouges addressed the crowd who gathered to watch. It was November, 1793, and the terrible period in France's history called the Reign of Terror had begun. Many thousands would lose their lives, as de Gouges did, to the guillotine, a machine named for the doctor who invented it as a way to quickly take off peoples' heads.

"Children of the Homeland," Olympe cried, "you shall avenge my death." Although this extraordinary woman's vision of equality was hundreds of years ahead of its time, she could not see that she stood almost alone in her foresight and courage. After her death, instead of being avenged, she was denounced and insulted. Some said her political activities showed she was insane. Her enemies said she should have kept to her place as a woman. Today, however, it is clear that Olympe de Gouges created history by writing an extensive document demanding women be given exactly the same rights as men. These demands are said to be the first of their kind; she made them more powerfully and completely than anyone else before. But she also recklessly challenged the political leaders of her time, which cost her her life.

There is little in Olympe's early years that explains or even hints at her future. She was born into a modest family as Marie Gouze in 1748, in a medieval town in southern France called Montauban. Her parents were Pierre Gouze, a butcher, and Anne-Olympe Mouisset. Marie had little or no education. Later, when she became a writer, she said, "I haven't the advantage of being schooled," although she actually was proud of what she called her "ignorance." She thought it allowed her to be more creative. She likely believed she was destined for a great future from a young age, as she was certain her real father was not Pierre, but a nobleman. Her mother was said to have had a love

Before Olympe

A few women in France and England argued for women's equality, although not as boldly as Olympe, starting as early as the 1400s.

- French philosopher Christine de Pisan (about 1365–1430) challenged negative ideas about women's abilities by writing about their accomplishments.

- A woman calling herself Jane Anger wrote the first feminist pamphlet in England in 1589. In it, she defended women's moral qualities, then considered inferior to men's.

- English philosopher Mary Astell (1666–1731) argued for education for women and criticized the inequalities of the institution of marriage for women in her time.

affair with the Marquis de Pompignan, a respected writer. There is no way to know if this was true, but Marie was convinced it was, although she was never officially recognized as the Marquis' child.

She married, at about seventeen, but was unhappy. She thought she was socially far superior to her husband, Louis-Yves Aubrey, who apparently worked as a servant. Marie's discontent is evident in a novel she wrote that was clearly based on her own life. The main character says her husband was "hateful"

Olympe de Gouges

to her. Nevertheless, a son, Pierre, was born to the Aubreys in 1766, the year after their marriage. Some biographers say Louis-Yves died soon after this; others suggest Marie left him. Whatever happened, after this date, Marie Aubrey changed her name to Olympe de Gouges, left for Paris, probably taking her son with her, and never married again.

Despite her lower-class upbringing and perhaps because of her beauty, Olympe became part of the high life of the city. She was involved with a wealthy businessman, Jacques Biéitrix de Villars de Rozières, who supported her financially. She wrote that she lived frivolously, spending "days dressing and beautifying myself." Still, Paris gave Olympe her first real education. She visited what were known as *salons*: fashionable gatherings of upper-class people for the purpose of conversations about everything from literature to politics.

In the 1700s, France was erupting with ideas from the period called the Enlightenment. The monarchy and the church, the most powerful institutions of the time, were being accused of oppression and there were cries for more freedom. Some also called for the freedom of black people who were slaves. Almost no one thought to include women in the new demands for liberty and equality. Most people believed, as one greatly admired male writer of the time said, that women should stay home and look after their men. They were "to be useful to us...to take care of us...to render our lives easy and agreeable."

Years later, an actor writing his memoirs about the salons described Olympe. His comments about her, and others, were often nasty. He claimed Olympe would fume if people didn't surround her to "bask in her radiance." But he also complimented her on her kindness and witty conversation and said she had "a keen eye and ear." Olympe took this talent and in 1784, when she had been in Paris at least fifteen years, became a published author. Perhaps because of her lack of education, her writing method was unique; she dictated her work to a stenographer who wrote it down it for her.

Olympe's writing drew attention to injustice, of all kinds. Through at least four novels, twelve plays, and the fifty short political pieces Olympe produced in her lifetime, she expressed bold opinions about what was unfair in society. She described herself as someone who would always "side with the weak and the oppressed." Her views were not popular and were often dismissed because she was female. One play she wrote, *L'Esclavage des nègres* or *Slavery of the Negroes*, portrayed slaves sympathetically and slavery as cruel. People thought it was immoral, and one reviewer said only men should be playwrights. "You've got to have a beard on the chin to write good dramatic work," he wrote. Olympe's play closed shortly after opening.

Some of Olympe's work may have been inspired by what she heard at the salons. In many cases, however, especially when it came to writing about women, it was as if she could actually see the future. Her dramas challenged stereotypes and the values of her time. She portrayed women living independently of men, and wrote a play about the necessity of divorce to save people from unhappy marriages. Divorce was rarely allowed in the 1700s.

Olympe began writing her political opinions in pamphlets, a popular way to publish one's views in 1788. Eventually, she would publish more about current events and politics than any other woman of that period. France was in trouble; the country was almost bankrupt and crop failures created famine and unrest. Olympe wrote pamphlets that suggested ways to help the economy. In June 1789, the turmoil became a crisis. A group representing the commoners of the country took control of an assembly that had been put together by King Louis XVI. This move attacked the authority of the the nobility and the church and, of course, the king, who had almost absolute power. The French Revolution had begun.

For a while, it seemed the king would go along with the newly named National Assembly, but actually he was buying time to put together military forces. By July, food shortages and the fear of attack by the king's forces brought tensions in Paris to a breaking point. On

Ahead of her time

Olympe understood many things we take for granted in the modern age – such as the importance of cleanliness. People thought she was odd because she took daily baths. She called for clean maternity hospitals so women could give birth in sanitary conditions; one in four women died in childbirth in existing facilities.

9

July 14, still celebrated today as a holiday in France, crowds in Paris stormed the Bastille, a fortress used as a prison. A battle erupted; dozens of Parisians were killed, and when the troops inside eventually surrendered, the crowd massacred several soldiers.

Afterward, King Louis XVI went to Paris, wearing the three-colored ribbons that symbolized the Revolution, indicating he would work with the new government. The world had never seen anything like it. Common people had defeated royalty.

Olympe continued writing during these first years of the Revolution, turning her eye to problems of basic human needs such as health and help for the elderly and unemployed. But her history-making moment was about to arrive.

In 1791, the government of the Revolution proclaimed its new constitution. Constitutions establish the fundamental principles on which a country is based. France's began with the *Déclaration des droits de l'homme et du citoyen*, the Declaration of the Rights of Man and of the Citizen. It heralded a new age, one in which people, not kings and queens, would rule. All men, it began, have the rights of freedom and equality. It then outlined other rights, including the right to political participation. But the document only gave *men* these rights. None of the new freedoms were given to women. The revolutionary government was as blind to women's abilities and rights as all previous regimes had been, despite the fact women had initiated, organized, and participated in many of the events that had created the Revolution.

Olympe went wild. She had written a lot of earlier work criticizing restrictions on women, but now they were talking about the constitution for a new way of government – and women were left out. Within days, she published and distributed her own document: *Déclaration des droits de la femme et de la citoyenne*, Declaration of the Rights of Woman and of the [Female] Citizen. She followed the structure and wording of the

Declaration of the Rights of Man. That document said, "Men are born and remain free and equal in rights," so Olympe wrote, "Woman is born free and remains equal to man in rights."

She followed this statement with fifteen articles claiming the same rights for women as men had in the constitution, including an equal voice in running the country and the right to own property. As for the law and opportunities for public positions and jobs, she wrote, "It must be the same for all." In her introduction, she asked men who had given them the right "to oppress my sex?" and said man "wants to rule" over women, even though women were equal to men intellectually. She also wrote, "Woman has the right to mount the scaffold; she must also have that of mounting the rostrum." A scaffold is a platform used when executing prisoners and a rostrum is a platform for public speaking. In other words, if women could be executed by their country, they should also have a voice in running their country.

Olympe's work was as revolutionary as the new government's. According to more than one historian, her demands that women be given full civic and political rights were the first of their kind and were broader than anything written previously. But there was barely any response, and the equal rights

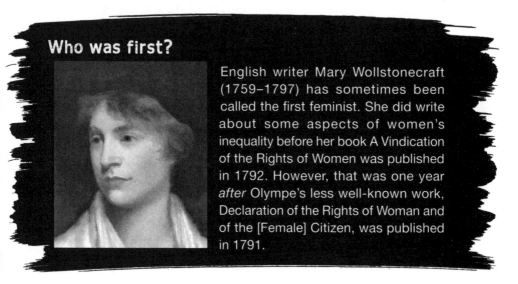

Who was first?

English writer Mary Wollstonecraft (1759–1797) has sometimes been called the first feminist. She did write about some aspects of women's inequality before her book A Vindication of the Rights of Women was published in 1792. However, that was one year *after* Olympe's less well-known work, Declaration of the Rights of Woman and of the [Female] Citizen, was published in 1791.

she called for would not be established for at least 150 years. In France, women were not given the right to vote until 1944.

There are many explanations for the lack of response in 1791. The most likely is that she was simply too far ahead of her time. Few people thought women, or women's rights, mattered. It may also have had something to do with the fact many people supporting the Revolution didn't like Olympe.

After 1789, she said she would not take sides between the nobility and those claiming to represent the people. "I know no party. The only one that really interests me is that of my homeland, that of France..." she wrote. She also believed change would be more peaceful if some form of monarchy, with reduced powers, was maintained. Olympe was opposed to violence and warned against it as the Revolution progressed – "Citizens, prepare yourselves for scaffolds and gallows to be erected in all of Paris' streets." She was right, yet again, although whether she foresaw her own death, we don't know.

September 1792 was to see the final turn of events against King Louis XVI and his Queen, Marie Antoinette. Mobs erupted and killed more than 1,000 people in prison for their politics. One woman killed was a close friend of the Queen's; her head was put on a pike and paraded before Marie Antoinette's windows. "Blood," Olympe wrote, "eternally soils these revolutions." Later that month, the Revolution's government officially abolished the monarchy.

Olympe now started down the path that would lead to her own execution. She wrote a pamphlet attacking Maximilien Robespierre, one of the revolutionary leaders involved with the more violent government party that was blamed for the September massacres. "Whose blood are you still thirsty for?" Olympe wrote about Robespierre. "You would like to make a path for yourself between the heaps of the dead..." Dangerous words in dangerous times.

In December, 1792, Louis XVI was put on trial for plotting against the Revolution. Ignoring popular opinion, Olympe pleaded for his life. She did not believe in capital punishment, and while acknowledging Louis had done wrong, she said his greatest "crime" was to have been born a king at the wrong time. "We have abolished royalty," she wrote. "His people, his throne: he's lost everything. Let us be good enough to leave him his life." No one listened. Louis was found guilty, and on January 21, 1793, the last king of France was taken to a Paris square, and tens of thousands watched as he was executed by guillotine.

Six months later, Olympe published and distributed another document. It called for the French people to have more choices in their government. This, finally, was her undoing. Robespierre was even more powerful, and in 1793 the government decreed rule by "Terror": it would silence its opposition through fear. The Reign of Terror lasted just ten months, but in that time some estimates say at least 300,000 people were arrested and 17,000 were executed. Many others died in prison without trial. Olympe was arrested in July and put on trial in early November, two weeks after Marie-Antoinette

Women in the Revolution

Women participated in almost every aspect of the French Revolution from its start. In October 1789, the Women's March on the King's palace at Versailles to protest high food prices became one of the uprising's most significant events. However, in October 1793, the new government outlawed some aspects of women's involvement in politics. And during the Reign of Terror, many women who had supported the revolution were imprisoned or executed. The woman known as Manon Roland, who had been a leading revolutionary figure, was one. She was guillotined just a few days after Olympe, in November 1793. Like Olympe, she got on the wrong side of Robespierre.

was guillotined. Olympe was found guilty of contempt of the laws, and beheaded.

After her death, one revolutionary warned women about getting involved in politics, writing that Olympe had been punished for "having forgotten the virtues that suit her sex." Today, Olympe de Gouges has at least some of the vengeance she called for. Scholars not only say that her Declaration is historic, but also that it laid the groundwork for the fights for women's votes and many other women's rights throughout the 20th century – battles that changed laws about women in society.

Still, there is always one more fight. In Paris, since 1791, the remains of France's greatest heroes have been laid to rest in the building called the Panthéon. More than two centuries later, only one woman had been buried there as the result of her own achievements: the scientist Marie Curie. There are seventy-five men in the Panthéon. Some women in France have held loud public demonstrations insisting that Olympe should be honored there as well. She would be pleased.

SOJOURNER TRUTH

**"I felt as if the power
of a nation was with me."**

1797 – 1883

Sojourner Truth, a former slave, was trying to give a speech at a college in Michigan one day during the American Civil War. The white students, like many people of the time, disdained black people, and they were showing it by hissing, pounding on their seats, and laughing. Sojourner, a majestic figure, six feet (1.8 meters) tall, kept her dignity. She told her hostile audience she had a question for them. "When you go to heaven," she said, "and God asks you what made you hate the colored people, have you got your answer ready?" She paused to let them think about that for a bit. Then she said, when God asks her, "Sojourner, what made you hate the white people?" she had her answer. Pulling the collar of her dress open, she showed them the network of scars made years earlier by a white slave master's whip.

Escaping slavery to fight it

Harriet Tubman (1820–1913) was another former slave who became a famous abolitionist. She escaped slavery in Maryland by fleeing to Pennsylvania. She continually risked her new freedom, however, by returning to slave states to help hundreds of others escape. At one time a reward of $40,000 was offered for Tubman's capture. Tubman and Sojourner met in Boston in 1864, where they talked about President Abraham Lincoln and his support for their anti-slavery crusade.

It is hard to imagine all that Sojourner Truth endured, and all she lost, in the first half of her life. Before she was born, her sister and brother were kidnapped and sold into slavery. Slavery, the cruel practice of people owning other people as pieces of property, had been in place in the United States since the 1600s. As a nine-year-old child, Sojourner, too, was taken from her parents and sold, and then sold twice more by the time she was thirteen. She was brutally worked for at least twenty years.

She never learned to read or write. Yet she became perhaps the most highly regarded African American woman of the nineteenth century, and is renowned today as a symbol of what one person can do to turn the world, as she said, "right side up."

She did it by trekking off into the unknown, guided only by her faith. Her gift was "talking aloud." Reporters who heard her said she had "a heart of love" and a "tongue of fire," and she used both as she traveled across most of the United States trying to persuade everyone to abolish slavery, and promote women's rights.

A number of well-known former slaves who fought for the abolition of slavery came from the South. Sojourner Truth came from a northern state. Slave births were not recorded, but it's believed she was born about 1797 in the village of

Hurley, about 90 miles (145 kilometers) north of New York City. Her parents, Elizabeth and James, named her Isabella. The first family that owned Isabella was Dutch, like many in New York State, so Dutch was her first language. The family that bought her when she was only nine spoke English, and the young girl was whipped because she could not understand them. She was sold around 1810 to a man named John Dumont. By now, Isabella had learned English, and at thirteen, had already reached her full height. She worked in the kitchen and fields; Dumont bragged she could do the work of six white people. Nevertheless, he beat her, which was considered perfectly normal.

When she was about eighteen, Isabella married Thomas, another of Dumont's slaves. Slave owners often made their slaves marry each other; their children then became the slave owner's property. Isabella had five children, but because they "belonged" to Dumont, she said she could never pick any of them up and say "my child" to them, unless she was sure no one could hear.

When Dumont sold her young son Peter, however, she confronted him in a landmark legal case. She had already fled the household in 1826, after sixteen years as the family's slave, when Dumont failed to live up to his promise to free her. Afterward, she discovered five-year-old Peter had been sold and was in Alabama. New York State's slave laws allowed for Peter to be sold in New York, but it was illegal for him to be taken elsewhere. At first, Isabella made a plea directly to the Dumonts, asking that her son be returned. They just scoffed at her.

Black people had little power to take on slave owners, but Isabella had a courage and determination that rose up in her whenever someone did something terribly wrong. "I was sure God would help me git him," she said later. "Why, I felt so *tall within* – I felt as if the power of a nation was with me." Advised by anti-slavery activists, she launched a lawsuit, and by the spring of 1827, Peter was returned to his mother. Isabella became one of the first black women to win a case in the U.S. courts.

Gradual changes in state laws, which now freed people according to their age, meant that Isabella was officially no longer a slave by 1828. She moved to New York City with Peter. Her other children were still legally enslaved, and had to remain behind. It seems she never saw her husband again; it's believed he died sometime later.

Isabella spent the next fourteen years in and around the city. She had some bad experiences; she spent three years in the company of religious fakers who took people's money. Eventually, she left them. But she was ecstatic when she met her sister and brother at a New York City church. They had been sold before she was born. Isabella began preaching in black churches during this period. Generally, this was not something women did; men were the ones considered to have the authority to spread the "Word of God." The effect of Isabella's preaching, however, was said to be "miraculous."

By 1843, working as a servant, Isabella had become unhappy with the direction of her life. As she later told the story, she asked "the Spirit" what to do, and a voice told her, "Go East." So, on June 1st that year, carrying only a pillowcase with a few clothes, Isabella began the walk that took her into a new life. She had no plan. She told her employer the Spirit had called her, "and I must go." Isabella took a new name: Sojourner – a word that describes someone without a home, who only stays in one place for a short time. She chose a new last name as well. As a former slave, she would have been known by the last name of her white owner. She chose the name Truth, because she wanted to speak God's truth.

After she left New York City, Sojourner preached from place to place. She was not yet speaking against slavery or women's rights, but her "tongue of fire" was evident. At one meeting where other preachers had whipped the crowd into a frenzy with talk of the world ending and life in the here-after, she scolded them. "Here you are talking about being 'changed in the twinkling of an eye.' If the Lord should come, he'd change you to *nothing*. For there is nothing to you. You seem to be expecting to go to some parlor *away up* somewhere, and when the wicked have been burnt, you are coming back to walk in triumph over their ashes...Now I can't see anything so very *nice* in that..."

In 1844, one year after she changed her life and her name, Sojourner joined a group of people who would change her again. The Northampton Association of Education and Industry, in Northampton, Massachusetts, was a commune of like-minded people living together. Its founders included abolitionists who also practiced values of equality between women and men. Sojourner learned from leaders of the anti-slavery movement who visited there, and met women working for women's rights.

Steeped in the ideas of Northampton, in 1845 Sojourner embarked on the mission that would make her a legend – preaching about slavery and women's rights. They were not com-pletely separate issues. Women had no right to property, or to vote and were subject to their hus-bands' rule – similar to slavery. One woman at that time said blacks and females were the "two most hated elements of

Black women preachers

While women of the 19th century did not usually preach, some African American women defied the rules to follow their calling. Like Sojourner, they traveled all over the countryside, and, because churches often wouldn't allow them in the pulpit, would preach in everything from tents, to clearings in the bush.

humanity." Sojourner was both, and her mission was risky; black people and anti-slavery activists were often attacked.

But Sojourner truly had a gift. People writing about her speeches said she melted away "the prejudice of color...we have seldom witnessed more marked results upon the Soul of an audience." How did she do it? By telling stories, with insights that opened people's minds, and with humor. Sometimes she'd make fun of herself. "Children," she said (she often called people "children" or "honey"), "I've come here like the rest of you to hear what I have to say." She also had a moving singing voice, and sometimes sang hymns. That was how, at one meeting, she subdued men who had come to attack people with clubs. After listening to Sojourner sing, they calmed down and went away.

She didn't always try to make peace with bullies, though. When some brutish men went to a women's rights convention, and were hissing at the speakers, including Sojourner, she called them geese and snakes, because they hissed. Then she said, "We'll have our rights; see if we don't; and you can't stop us from them; see if you can. You may hiss as much as you like, but it is coming."

Sojourner's most famous speech took place at another women's rights convention in Akron, Ohio, in May of 1851. Debates raged; some women thought it was important to get the vote; others thought that was too radical. One clergyman told all the women to go home to their husbands. The first day, Sojourner just listened quietly to the arguments. On the second day, she asked if she could speak.

The reports of her exact words vary. The records come from newspapers and essays, but the essays were written years later, and the reports say different things. There is no doubt, however, that she was powerful. Her unique thoughts and expressions are the reasons the speech is remembered and quoted to this day. She took the arguments used against women, and women's rights, turned them upside down, and demolished them.

Some people argued the reason women shouldn't speak, preach, and weren't equal to men was because Jesus Christ, the son of God, was a man. But Sojourner asked, "And how came Jesus into the world?" Her audience knew the Bible said that Jesus was born of the Virgin Mary, who was pregnant through the Holy Spirit. Well, Sojourner replied, that meant Jesus came from "God and a woman. Man had not'ing to do with him."

Others argued that women were weak and, therefore, men should be in charge. But speaking of her slave days, Sojouner said, "I have plowed and reaped and husked and chopped and mowed, and can any man do more than that?" The Akron speech came to be known by the name "Arn't I a Woman?" (or, sometimes, "Ain't I a Woman?"), because she repeated this question each time she pointed out that she was no different than men, and she deserved equal rights: "I could work as much and eat as much as a man – when I could get it – and bear the lash as well! And arn't I a woman?"

At this time, Sojourner was about fifty-four years old. She preached in twenty-one states and one district, and her fame grew with each appearance. It grew even more when her life was made into a book, the *Narrative of Sojourner Truth.* In Northampton, she had dictated her story to a female friend, and when it was finally published in 1850, the money it earned helped Sojourner buy her first home in Massachusetts.

When America's Civil War broke out on April 12, 1861, Sojourner continued traveling and speaking out against slavery, despite the risks. She went to Indiana, for example, where the so-called Black Laws limited black people's rights to be in the state. She was arrested several times and threatened, but eventually was let go. She also worked with black troops fighting on the Northern side, against the eleven Southern states that wanted to keep slavery, and to secede – to separate – from the other states in the Union.

Increasing fame

Writer Harriet Beecher Stowe was another reason Sojourner's fame continued to spread. Stowe was the author of the highly popular anti-slavery novel, Uncle Tom's Cabin. Stowe was not only an abolitionist, but also a supporter of women's rights, and Sojourner influenced her. An article Stowe wrote about Sojourner was published in 1863 in the Atlantic Monthly. It included many inaccuracies, but served as another tool to draw attention to Sojourner's causes.

In 1863, although the war was not over yet, President Abraham Lincoln signed the Emancipation Proclamation, freeing millions of slaves. The Proclamation could not be enforced in areas still fighting Northern forces, but thousands of those who had been freed poured into Washington. There was no food or jobs for them, and the only place they had to live were refugee camps. Sojourner went to Washington in 1864 to help. She said she didn't have words to describe what she saw: the "rags and wretchedness and hunger and poverty." Sojourner also met with President Lincoln that year and thanked him for what he had done for her people. The meeting was later commemorated in a painting of the famous pair.

The war ended in 1865 and American slavery ended with it. But discrimination and the poor conditions of black people continued. By then in her seventies, Sojourner campaigned against both. She took a streetcar conductor to court for injuring her when he threw her off his car – like many drivers, he didn't want black people to ride with whites. In 1870, she met President Ulysses S. Grant and spoke to him about giving black people free land. She said it would help pay back former slaves for all the free labor and profits their owners had benefitted from for so long.

Nothing happened with this proposal, and the issue of what are called reparations – compensation for the damage of slavery – has been raised repeatedly since that time.

Sojourner continued to travel and speak out publicly for African Americans and women well into her eighties. She said women should have the right to be paid the same as a man for doing the same work and should have the right to

Abraham Lincoln and Sojourner Truth, Washington, D.C. ,1864.

vote. In 1872, although it was illegal for women, she tried to vote in the presidential election. She was turned away. She died November 26, 1883, at about age eighty-six, in Michigan. During her final illness, she told a friend she wasn't going to die. Instead, she said, "I'm going home like a shooting star."

Slavery had been practiced for more than two centuries in the United States when it ended. The woman formerly known as Isabella might have disappeared into history, like so many others who bore its wretched existence. Instead, she took a forty-year journey dedicated to ending suffering and opening people's lives to new freedoms. In 2009, in Washington, she became the first black woman honored with a statue in the Capitol, the seat of the United States government. The statue was unveiled by Michelle Obama, a descendant of slaves and wife of the first African American president of the United States.

The women's vote

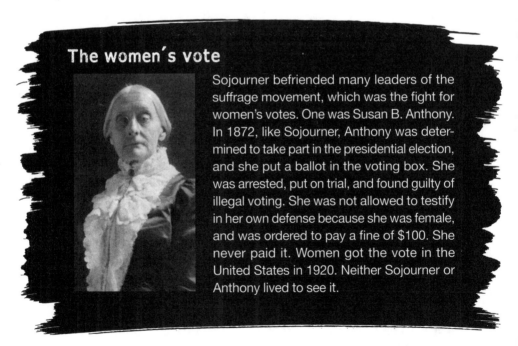

Sojourner befriended many leaders of the suffrage movement, which was the fight for women's votes. One was Susan B. Anthony. In 1872, like Sojourner, Anthony was determined to take part in the presidential election, and she put a ballot in the voting box. She was arrested, put on trial, and found guilty of illegal voting. She was not allowed to testify in her own defense because she was female, and was ordered to pay a fine of $100. She never paid it. Women got the vote in the United States in 1920. Neither Sojourner or Anthony lived to see it.

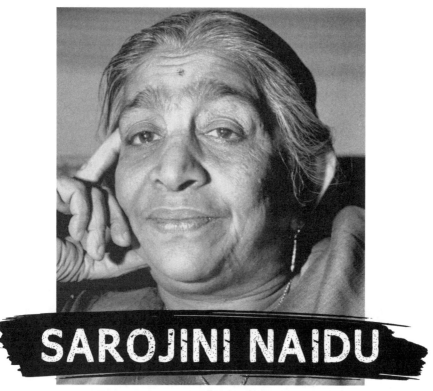

SAROJINI NAIDU

**"You deserve no Empire.
You have. . . lost your soul."**
1879 – 1949

There was little about Sarojini Naidu that appeared revolutionary. She was a poet who loved to dress in colorful clothes and clinging silk saris. She was described as speaking in a low, musical voice and as being so small "you might have taken her for a child." Yet Sarojini was courageous enough to stand weaponless before enemies who were armed. She was confident and calm enough when she was being arrested to shrug off the official's hand with a smile and a warning: "Don't touch me." She was tough enough to endure numerous times in jail. She did all this because she had an unwavering belief she must free her country from the rule of those she said had become "blind and drunk" with power. In the end, she helped overthrow the world's mightiest empire.

Sarojini was born February 13, 1879, in Hyderabad, India. Her father, Aghornath Chattopadhyaya, was a scientist and educator, and her mother, Varada Sundari, wrote poetry. Sarojini was the eldest of eight children in a house described by her brother as a "cross between a museum and a zoo." It was full of animals, and a strange mix of visitors, from wandering singers to professors, beggars, and priests. Aghornath, while greatly admired by many for his intellect and politics, was also somewhat odd. He carried out experiments in alchemy, trying to turn common metals into gold. The family was Hindu and spoke two Indian languages, Urdu and Telegu, as well as English.

From the time she was young, Sarojini suffered periods of poor health. However, she was an exceptional student; when she was only twelve, she passed examinations equivalent to completing high school, with top results. She was away from home for these studies, but returned afterward, partly because of illness. There, she continued her early interest in poetry writing. Still, the family worried about Sarojini: she had fallen in love – and she was only about fifteen years old.

Govindarajulu Naidu was much older than Sarojini and had just finished medical college. He was also from a different caste. For Hindus, your place in society, for your whole life, was determined by what caste, or group, you were born into, and it was illegal at that time to marry outside it. Sarojini's father was Brahmin, the highest caste. Some said caste difference was the reason her parents sent Sarojini overseas. Others say they simply thought she was too young for such a serious relationship. In September, 1895, at age sixteen, Sarojini sailed to England to go to university.

England was the center of the British Empire, the largest empire in history. It ruled colonies and territories around the world, including India. Achieving India's freedom would become Sarojini's life work, for which she would travel to England many more times, but as a teenager, she was mostly interested in poetry. She spent time with literary people, worked on her writing, and seemed to have little interest in her studies. She returned to India in 1898, and married the man she still loved, Govindarajulu, that year. They had to marry in a non-religious ceremony to avoid the law preventing marriages between castes.

Over the next several years, the Naidus had four children. Sarojini continued to write, and her first volume of poetry, *The Golden Threshold*, published in 1905, received good reviews. Sarojini was encouraged to be herself – be Indian – in her poems. This first collection, and all those that followed, reflected that advice. A biographer later said, every line "has the flavor of India, just as every drop of the ocean has the taste of salt." Many of her poems were about the people of India: farmers, snake-charmers, and traveling singers – the type of people she would have met as a child.

In her early twenties, Sarojini got involved in politics through an organization called the Indian National Congress. The Congress became a major force in the movement to rid India of British control. Britain had ruled India in one form

The caste system

When Sarojini turned to a political life, she campaigned against the caste system, and especially the degrading treatment of people called Untouchables. There are four castes, Brahmin (priests/scholars), Kshatriya (warriors/nobles), Vaishya (agriculturists/merchants), and Shudra (artisans/laborers). Untouchables are a fifth group, considered the lowest of the low. India's new constitution outlawed discrimination on the basis of caste in 1950, but the system has existed for more than 2,000 years, and its influence remains forceful today. Untouchables suffer continuing prejudice that denies them access to education and forces them into the filthiest and worst jobs. Marriage between castes, although no longer illegal, also remains taboo.

or another for more than a century, but growing numbers of Indians wanted the British out. They believed the British were making themselves rich on India's wealth of natural resources while Indians were kept poor. British rule discriminated against Indians at the same time as it forced them to pay unfair taxes.

In 1904, Sarojini attended a Congress meeting in Bombay, where participants discussed Britain and also the problems facing Indian women. Girls often weren't educated, and child marriages were common; girls as young as five years old could be forcibly married to older men. There was also the problem of purdah, which greatly limited women's lives by preventing them from being seen in public. Sarojini was developing a vision for India that freed it from Britain, but also challenged the restrictions on Indian girls and women.

Child marriages

The United Nations' first International Day of the Girl Child was marked in 2012 by calling for an end to child marriages. Although often illegal, it is still practiced today in more than 50 developing countries. The UN says young girls forced to marry, often to men decades older, suffer health effects from becoming pregnant too early, are denied basic rights such as education, and are frequently subject to abuse. A UN program focusing on some of the places with the worst abuses of child marriage included India, Guatemala, Niger, and Zambia.

An influential Congress leader encouraged Sarojini to devote her life to the service of her country. She began her political career with public speaking, often to groups of students. She spoke about independence, bettering women's lives, and also about ridding India of religious hatred. Two main religious groups, Muslims and Hindus, had conflicts going back centuries. Sarojini told them if they did not end their prejudices against one another, they would never be a nation.

In 1914, Sarojini met the man who matched her ideals for the future of India with a method to achieve them. Still suffering poor health, she had returned for a time to England. In London, she met Mohandas Gandhi, also called the Mahatma, which means "great soul." Gandhi was born Hindu in India, but two other religions, Jainism and Christianity, also influenced him in developing a protest method called *satyagraha*. Satyagraha is loosely translated as "insistence on truth," and it emphasized non-violence. Peaceful protesters broke laws they believed unjust, and were arrested, as a way of drawing attention to their struggles. They sometimes risked physical attack from police or other authorities but refused to fight back. Sarojini said Gandhi's plan was to free India with a weapon that "was not the machine-gun or the sword but the... weapon of spiritual revolt." She worked with Gandhi for more than thirty years, leading one of the most important satyagraha campaigns herself.

Sarojini returned to India in 1915, where she would mourn the loss of both her parents – her father that year and her mother in 1916. Then a tragedy in the city of Amritsar, in northern India, brought her to a new level of despair, leading her to tell the British, "You deserve no Empire. You have...lost your soul."

In 1919, the British introduced harsh laws, aimed at the Indian independence movement, that allowed them to arrest and confine anyone suspected of working against British rule. Gandhi, now back in India, called for a satyagraha against these laws. Sarojini was one of the first to support him, urging people to resist the "hideous nightmare." Then, on April 13, 1919, British troops fired on an unarmed crowd of protesters in Amritsar. More than 300 people were killed.

Sarojini returned to England to meet with British authorities about Amritsar, this time as a representative of the Home Rule League, an organization dedicated to Indian independence.

But all the British did was issue an official criticism of the commander in charge of the troops who had fired. Sarojini was devastated by their lack of action. In a letter to Gandhi she said it "shattered the last remnants of my hope and faith in British justice…"

Throughout the 1920s, Sarojini's value to the independence movement continued to grow. She was elected President of the Indian National Congress in 1925, the first woman to take this post. It was an accomplishment noted around the world. The highly influential *New York Times* newspaper compared her to Joan of Arc, who had led the French army into battle against English troops centuries earlier. She traveled as a type of ambassador, promoting Indian independence in the United States, Canada, and other places.

In India, there were more campaigns against Britain, with thousands arrested. Gandhi spent two years in jail, from 1922 to 1924. Sarojini's political partnership and friendship with him continued to grow, although in style, they were very different. He led what some would say was an austere life. He only wore rough homespun Indian cotton, believing in the value of plain, simple things, and in using local goods rather than ones purchased from Britain. He was also vegetarian. Sarojini, on the other hand, loved to wear colorful silk, and as to being vegetarian, she said, "Good heavens! Grass and goat's milk? Never!" Her admiration for Gandhi was boundless; she called him a saint, and meant it. But she also liked to make fun, calling him Mickey Mouse, a cartoon character with big ears, and "little man." Their relationship was one of great mutual respect, warmth, and humor.

The start of a new decade would see Gandhi develop another campaign that would have an impact across the country and, indeed, around the world. This time, Sarojini would be front and center. The new satyagraha was about making salt.

Salt was essential for everyday cooking. Yet Britain taxed it heavily, making it expensive for Indians, especially the poor, to buy. At the same time, British laws did not allow Indians to make their own salt. Gandhi decided to break this law, announcing he would lead seventy *sataygrahi* – peaceful protesters – on a march to the sea, where they would use seawater to produce salt. Protesting British rule with salt-making seems almost silly, and both the British and some in the Congress party thought it was odd. But it was actually a stroke of genius because it affected so many people's lives. On March 12, 1930, the protesters set out from western India, where Gandhi lived, to walk 240 miles (385 kilometers) to Dandi on the Arabian Sea. At each stop along their march, hundreds more joined them.

Initially, no women were in the group. Sarojini determined she would join the protest, and she was joined by thousands more. The marchers reached Dandi on April 5, 1930, and after a night of prayer, they went into the sea to collect salt water. Sarojini's sister-in-law described the scene of women striding "down to the sea like proud warriors. But instead of weapons, they bore pitchers of clay, brass and copper." The protesters then made salt, and afterwards, breaking the law further, sold what they made. "We have broken the laws and we are free," they cried. Who will buy the salt of freedom?"

Women and the Salt March

The Salt March marked a new level of women's participation in India's independence movement.

The British laws about salt affected their everyday lives. The salt protest spread across the country, largely because of women who not only made the illegal salt, but also sold it in marketplaces. The march is considered to be the first time masses of Indian women from all classes joined the struggle opposing Britain.

Thousands were arrested. On May 5th, Gandhi was as well. But another salt march had already been planned, and so Sarojini became the leader. About 2,500 protesters, all dedicated to non-violent action, went to the Dharasana Salt Works, north of Bombay. When they tried to take down fences around the factory's salt fields, the police attacked them. Sarojini told her people, "You will be beaten but you must not resist." Satyagraha required they not use force under any circumstances.

A reporter later said the scene of peaceful people being "bashed into a bloody pulp sickened me so much I had to turn away." He also described Sarojini's arrest. "One of the British officials approached her, touched her on the arm, and said: 'Sarojini Naidu, you are under arrest.' She laughingly shook off his hand and said, 'I'll come, but don't touch me.'"

Her response to arrest always seemed calm. On another occasion, an observer described her sitting in a rocking chair on the street, wearing a colorful sari, waiting for the police van to come and take her away. For Dharasana, she would be in jail about seven months. In total, the salt protests put about 60,000 people behind bars by the end of that year.

The head of the British administration in India made light of what happened when he wrote to the King. Although a reporter said he had seen people at the hospital with fractured skulls, and in agony from being kicked, Lord Irwin wrote, "Your Majesty can hardly fail to have read with amusement the accounts of...Dharasana." He claimed there were only "minor injuries."

While the British leader may not have taken it seriously, the protest had many important consequences. The people of India had sent a message they were willing to suffer and be jailed in order to win freedom. And world newspapers took notice, describing "a great revolutionary movement" that was "sweeping through India." Britain was forced to talk about

Indian self-rule and after their release from jail, Sarojini and Gandhi returned to England in 1931 for a new round of discussions.

It would be another sixteeen years before Britain finally gave up power in India. In 1942, during World War II, Gandhi organized his last country-wide satyagraha. It was called the "Quit India" campaign, but as soon as it was announced, Gandhi and Sarojini were arrested. Eventually tens of thousands of others were also arrested and imprisoned. Sarojini was in jail for almost two years, where she spent time cooking for other prisoners and planting flowers.

In 1947, independence was achieved, but at a cost. Sarojini and Gandhi had hoped to achieve Hindu-Muslim unity in an independent India. This ideal was lost to the act of partition, which divided the country into two nations – Pakistan, where Muslims were the majority, and India, where Hindus were the majority. There was a period of terrible violence. As many as one million people were killed in riots and fighting.

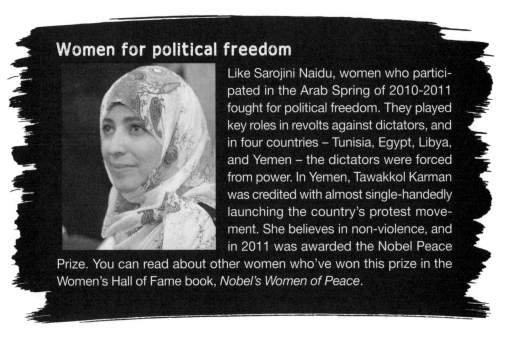

Women for political freedom

Like Sarojini Naidu, women who participated in the Arab Spring of 2010-2011 fought for political freedom. They played key roles in revolts against dictators, and in four countries – Tunisia, Egypt, Libya, and Yemen – the dictators were forced from power. In Yemen, Tawakkol Karman was credited with almost single-handedly launching the country's protest movement. She believes in non-violence, and in 2011 was awarded the Nobel Peace Prize. You can read about other women who've won this prize in the Women's Hall of Fame book, *Nobel's Women of Peace*.

Gandhi tried to stop the bloodshed, but less than six months after independence, he was assassinated by a Hindu fanatic.

Sarojini was devastated, but continued her work for India. She became its first woman governor, of the state of Uttar Pradesh, which had a population of Hindus and Muslims. She died one year after Gandhi, of a heart attack, on March, 2, 1949. She was seventy.

When she was only fourteen, Sarojini wrote a poem that ended, "high ideas formed my radiant dream." Her life was devoted to the high ideal of an independent India, and her devotion was honored by thousands who gathered to watch her body be cremated on the side of a river in a customary Hindu funeral. While her idea of religious unity was not achieved, and her hopes for the caste system and many freedoms for women still have not been realized, Sarojini Naidu's work helped upturn an empire, and she did this using non-violent methods. The example set by the satyagrahas inspired many great reform movements that followed, including the 1960s' civil rights movement.

What the small woman in the silk sari never lost was her grace. After her death, Jawaharlal Nehru, India's first prime minister, honored this quality. He said Sarojini faced disaster "with a light heart, with a song on her lips and a smile on her face." She lived her life so beautifully, he said, her whole life was a poem.

RUTH FIRST

"South Africa belongs to all who live in it, black and white."

1925 – 1982

Joe Slovo always knew he or his wife, Ruth First, might die violently. Their life's work was fighting the South African government and police system that had already jailed, tortured, and murdered others who opposed them. Joe warned Ruth, "Never open the door if you don't know who is on the other side," and told her to be careful opening mail. Bombs placed inside letters were a known assassination technique.

On August 17, 1982, Joe received a call from a friend at Ruth's office at Eduardo Mondlane University in Maputo, Mozambique. "Come quickly," the friend said, "something has happened." He sped to the building and ran up the stairs where he found a crowd of people and the ruin left by an exploded bomb. Sticking out from behind the remains of her

Ruth's daughters

A normal relationship with her children was one of many sacrifices Ruth made. After their mother's death, two of Ruth's daughters told the story of their parents' life, and its impact on them. Gillian Slovo wrote an international bestseller, *Every Secret Thing: My Family, My Country*. Shawn Slovo wrote a successful feature film called *A World Apart*. Both depicted difficult childhoods with activist parents, who worked in a dangerous time and place. The children always had to keep things secret, were taught not to trust anyone, and often didn't even know where their parents were.

desk, Joe saw Ruth's feet, clad in her favorite shoes. He knew from her stillness she was dead.

Ruth First was fifty-seven years old when a letter bomb sent by the South African police killed her. For more than thirty years, her goal had been to rid her country of the evil called apartheid, a cause that mattered to her above all else. In South Africa, apartheid laws gave whites all the power, although black people made up the majority of the population. Joe and Ruth were white, but they were unlike most South Africans of their race. They believed apartheid was wrong. Ruth was willing to suffer anything, and did, to have the racist system abolished: imprisonment, the loss of normal family life, exile, and finally, death. In the end, her work and others' defeated apartheid's injustice.

Ruth lived outside the norms and values of most white South Africans, even as a child. She was born May 4, 1925, in Johannesburg, to Julius and Matilda (Tilly) First. They were Jewish, which meant they had experienced anti-Semitism, although it was not as severe in South Africa as the discrimination of northeastern Europe, which they had left in the early 1900s. Julius was able to establish a furniture business in Johannesburg, which gave the family a comfortable living. Their passion, however, was politics. They belonged to the Communist Party – one of the few political groups to include black members and to call for black people to run the government. Apartheid was not in place when Ruth was a child, but the country was strongly racist, and non-whites suffered great inequalities. Being Communist made the Firsts unusual, to say the least. "We didn't have ordinary friends," Tilly said. Most people feared and hated Communists. Ruth and her younger brother Ronald grew up attending political meetings with their parents.

At school, Ruth stood out as someone who was smart and well-spoken. A high school friend described her as "brilliant," but also realized she was timid. "I learned early that... she was very shy, private, she hid herself behind those dark glasses she always wore." Ruth excelled at the University of Witwatersrand as well, where she took African History and English. In the early 1940s, the university was integrated, with students from all races. Ruth met an Indian law student and activist there, and they had a four-year relationship, although interracial couples were uncommon, and generally frowned upon. Later, apartheid would make interracial marriage illegal. It also closed the university to non-whites.

Ruth graduated in 1946 and got a job writing and researching with the Johannesburg City Council. She quit soon after to help support a historic strike by black workers who mined South Africa's gold, under dangerous conditions. They were poorly paid, while the white owners grew rich. The conflict became violent; police beat and shot the strikers. More than 1,000 were injured, at least nine were killed, and the strike was quickly defeated.

When it was over, Ruth became a journalist, writing for small newspapers that shared her political views. She became known for her investigative work, uncovering stories about brutality and corruption. She discovered, for example, that police were arresting black men for minor offences, then turning them over to white farm owners who forced them to work for free. Ruth's report sparked a protest against the farmers, which helped reduce the practice. Journalism was an important tool in Ruth's activism, and she would continue writing about racism and politics in articles and books until she died.

In 1948, when Ruth was twenty-three, she began her relationship with Joe Slovo. Joe had a different upbringing from Ruth. His parents had little money, and at fourteen, he left school to work. He fought in World War II, then returned to South Africa and became a lawyer. Friends say Ruth and Joe were opposites in personality. He was easygoing and self-confident. She was often insecure, and said to be difficult and demanding sometimes, although also "very loved." Both were committed Communists, and their political beliefs and activism united them. By 1949 they were living together, and when Ruth became pregnant, they decided to marry. Different as always, Ruth did not take her husband's last name, which was the common thing to do then. They had three daughters: Shawn, born in 1950, Gillian born in 1952, and Robyn in 1953.

The year before their marriage, a group called the National Party (NP) won South Africa's election. It had promised to make white voters even more powerful by strengthening racial segregation, and following its victory in 1948, the party immediately began putting apartheid in place. The goal was simple: to completely seal off anyone who wasn't white from anyone who was, and to give white people all the privileges and control.

Every South African was classified according to race, and race governed everything, from where you were allowed to work, to where you could live, and even who you could visit. There were four categories: Bantu for black Africans, Colored for those of mixed race, Asian for people of Indian and Pakistani origin, and White. Earlier laws had greatly restricted land owner-ship by black people and apartheid maintained this practice: at least eighty percent of the land was in the hands of white people, although in num-bers, whites made up only about twenty percent of the population. The NP created areas where only white people could live, own property, or have businesses and forced black people to move. If non-whites visited a white area, they had to have

The meaning of apartheid

Apartheid means "apartness" in the Afrikaner language of South Africa. Afrikaners are descen-dants of white European settlers from the Netherlands, Germany, and France. They make up the majority of the country's white population. There are also English-speaking white people descended from British settlers. All whites enjoyed the special powers apartheid gave them.

passes proving they had permission to be there. Non-whites were not allowed to hold government positions, and all eco-nomic advantages were given to whites.

Few whites protested. Ruth and Joe did. In her book about her parents' life, Gillian Slovo said most of their race were too happy with the opportunities apartheid gave them to get rich; they weren't going to worry about what was happening to black South Africans. "Not so my parents," she wrote. Joe and Ruth "broke all the rules" of apartheid, even though the government cracked down harshly on opposition. The more the government did to stop them, Gillian says, "the more they fought back."

For more than a decade, the activists' fight took the form of peaceful protests, designed to draw attention to the injus-tice of apartheid. One action, launched in 1952, was called the Defiance Campaign; some say it was the largest non-violent resistance movement the country had ever seen. It was organized by the African National Congress (ANC), which was dedicated to the rights of non-whites. During the protests, Ruth and Joe supported their friend, the ANC's Nelson Mandela, whom Ruth had met in university. The campaign called for people to refuse to obey unjust laws, such as carrying passes. The government responded by putting 8,000 people in jail and bringing in more laws, this time to stop people from protesting.

The government was constantly creating new ways to silence people who opposed them. The Communist Party was multiracial, and spoke out against apartheid, so in 1950, it was made illegal and was banned. Banning, and especially the banning of individuals, was a system almost completely unique to South Africa. The government banned people if it didn't like their political activities, banned them from taking part in those activities, and also put restrictions on where they could go and who they could meet. Books, magazines, and newspapers opposed to the government were banned, and police often raided activists' homes, searching for illegal publications or other evidence of anything that broke apartheid's laws.

Ruth received the first of what would be several banning orders against her in 1951. But she continued to work openly with the ANC and other anti-apartheid groups. One of her accomplishments was helping put together the historic Freedom Charter. The Charter began by declaring "...for all our country and the world to know: South Africa belongs to all who live in it, black and white, and that no government can justly claim authority unless it is based on the will of the people."

Three thousand anti-apartheid activists met in June of 1955 to adopt the Charter as their guiding principles for a nonracial South Africa. As the meeting wrapped up, the police, armed with machine guns, swept in, seized documents, and recorded the names of everyone there. Because they were banned, Ruth and Joe hadn't attended.

They were rounded up in another police raid on December 5, 1956. A total of 156 people were taken to prison and charged with treason – betraying their country. Mandela and others in the ANC were also arrested and charged with plotting to use violence to overthrow the government. Ruth and Joe's daughter Gillian said that the morning after the raid, newspaper reporters came and took pictures of her and her sisters having breakfast. Six-year-old Shawn told them, "Mummy's gone to prison to look after the black people." Eventually, all the accused were acquitted, and the judge said there was no proof of any plans for violence.

The activists' commitment to non-violent methods changed after the events of March 21, 1960, at a place called Sharpeville. On that day, thousands of protesters from all over the country were taking part in a new anti-pass campaign, breaking the law, but peacefully, by marching to police stations without their passes. In Sharpeville, police responded by opening fire on the crowd. Estimates said sixty-nine people were killed and nearly 200 wounded.

The United Nations and countries around the world condemned South Africa. The government didn't care. It thought the protesters deserved what they got and cracked down once again, declaring the country was in a state of emergency. It banned the ANC and other political groups. Police raided activists' homes in the middle of the night. They arrested Joe. Sure they would come back for her, Ruth packed up the children and fled into hiding. Months later, Joe was released, and they all returned home to Johannesburg, knowing, as Gillian said, that "nothing would ever be the same again."

She was right. Anti-apartheid leaders, seeing what had happened at Sharpeville, decided peaceful demonstrations would not accomplish their goals. Nelson Mandela and Joe Slovo became commanders of a new secret and illegal military wing of the ANC called *Umkhonto We Sizwe*, meaning "Spear of the Nation" in Zulu. It used armed force against the government and bombed its property and services. Mandela was determined people should not be killed during their operations, although over the next several decades, there were deaths. Mandela's purpose was to disrupt the government, compelling it to talk to the activists and change its policies. Umkhonto We Sizwe said South Africa was responsible for its adopting the use of force, because the government had "rejected every peaceable demand by the people for its rights and freedom and answered every such demand with force and more force!" Ruth believed the change was absolutely necessary; a decade later she wrote that apartheid was so wrong, "there is no way to change it but by destroying it."

So much of what Ruth and Joe were doing was now illegal, they couldn't tell their own children about it. Gillian says "secrecy drifted over every section of our lives." Ruth was "central to nearly everything" in the movement, according to an ANC activist, and this meant taking part in many illegal political meetings. One well-known South African novelist and activist described seeing her once on an airplane, tearing up papers that must have included evidence the authorities could use against her, and then taking the pieces and flushing them down the toilet.

On July 11, 1963, police raided a farmhouse in a suburb of Johannesburg called Rivonia. They found evidence of sabotage plans, and arrested many members of Umkhonto We Sizwe. Mandela was already under arrest, and he and several others were put on trial in October. International outcry against South Africa helped prevent the death penalty, but in 1964 he, along with seven others, was sentenced to life in prison with no possibility of parole.

Joe Slovo escaped capture through pure luck. He had left town on a mission before the Rivonia raid. Afterward, he couldn't return without facing arrest, so went to live in England, leaving Ruth and the children alone in Johannesburg. On August 9, 1963, Ruth was arrested. Her daughters came home from school to find the police turning their house upside down, and their mother packing a suitcase. The police put Ruth in a car and drove away, leaving the girls with their grandmother.

It was certainly the most difficult time of Ruth's life. Joe Slovo said the police practiced their "skills" of mental torture on her. South Africa's law allowed police to hold Ruth without access to legal help or contact with anyone on the outside, and even without informing anyone of where she was. She was kept in solitary confinement, isolated from other prisoners. Ruth was haunted by fears of what was happening to her children and terrified she would give away secrets about other activists that would cause their arrest, or worse. She knew about the operations of Umkhonto We Sizwe, and had been to the Rivonia farmhouse almost daily before the raids. Her anxiety that she would betray people under repeated police questionings led Ruth to attempt suicide by taking pills, but the dose wasn't strong enough, and she survived.

After 117 days, the police released her. She didn't know why they let her go, but she was sure they would arrest her again. Still, she was reluctant to leave the country, wanting to stay and

117 days

After moving to England, Ruth wrote the bestselling book *117 Days*, a record of her nearly four months in a South African jail. She wrote nine books about African politics, but this one was personal. One journalist said it portrayed "a woman on the edge. She fears she will crack..." Joe Slovo said she wasn't trying to draw attention to herself, but to make the world pay attention to the victims of South Africa's "physical and mental torture-machine." The book was made into a movie that, together with her writing, exposed millions to the cruelties of the South African government and police.

continue the fight. But the South African government, for the time being, had won. The Rivonia trials had mostly silenced the opposition by putting its leaders in jail. Ruth was almost entirely on her own. She applied for the documents she needed to move abroad, and left with her daughters on March 14, 1964, to join Joe in England. Ruth would never set foot in South Africa again.

From that time until her death, Ruth never stopped campaigning against apartheid. She wrote books, including the one about her time in prison. She also taught, and in 1977 was appointed research director at Eduardo Mondlane University in Maputo, Mozambique, a country neighboring South Africa. Mozambique had a new government and was a good place for her and Joe to continue their work.

It was also dangerous. In 1981 there was a raid against ANC people living in Maputo, and at least a dozen were killed. Ruth was worried about Joe, because he still worked for Umkhonto We Sizwe. But in the end, she was the one murdered. Some reports say the South African policemen assigned to kill her celebrated when they heard of her death.

Before she died, when Nelson Mandela was still in jail, Ruth wrote an introduction to his book *No Easy Walk to Freedom*. Although he was in prison, she said, Mandela continued to have "the confidence, the strength and the moral authority...that will, in time, bring the apartheid system toppling down." She was right. On February 11, 1990, after twenty-six years, Mandela was released and worked together with South Africa's president, Frederik Willem de Klerk, to end apartheid. In 1993, the two men won the Nobel Peace Prize for what they had done, and in 1994, the ANC won the first election in which all people had the right to vote. Mandela became president. Joe Slovo became minister of housing in the country's first multiracial government.

In the new South Africa, the Truth and Reconciliation Commission, headed by Anglican Archbishop Desmond Tutu, investigated the crimes of the former regime. The commission became a model of merciful justice to the world. Its purpose wasn't to punish but to record evidence of the crimes that had been committed because of racism. Anyone who gave a truthful and public account of what they had done would be given a pardon and forgiveness. Craig Williamson, the man who ordered the bomb that killed Ruth, and the man who actually made it, Roger Jerry Raven, gave their testimony and after much deliberation by the Commission were given amnesty.

The path to freedom for millions of South Africans was paved, in part, by Ruth First. After her death, a fellow activist said, "There's not a single important decision of the movement in the last thirty years that doesn't bear her imprint in some way." Joe said while the outside world saw his wife as strong and confident, she often suffered self-doubt. She never overcame uncertainties about what she had achieved. In one letter she wrote Joe in prison, she talked about what she thought made a "real hero." Heroes struggled, she said, and had an unbreakable spirit.

It was clear she didn't think of herself as heroic. Yet there is no doubt that is what South Africans and people around the world think of her today. In 2010, her old high school established an award in her name. The school motto, they noted, states that "for the brave, nothing is too difficult." Could anyone, they asked, have been a better example of this than Ruth First?

GLORIA STEINEM

"I've yet to hear a man ask for advice on how to combine marriage and a career."

1934 –

In March 1969, Gloria Steinem was in her mid-thirties, a successful writer and journalist living in New York City. Beautiful and glamorous, she had her own column in a popular magazine and a high profile in the media, socializing with the city's most fashionable people. Magazines such as *Newsweek* wrote stories about the "striking brunette" and the prominent men she dated. She was involved in numerous political causes, from protesting the United States' war in Vietnam to helping bring attention to the cause of poor agricultural laborers.

She was not, however, a feminist – until one day, as part of her magazine job, she attended a feminist event. Then everything changed in the way Gloria Steinem saw the world. She saw that women were subject to laws and a culture dominated by men, and were unequal to men in almost every aspect of their lives. From that point forward, she devoted herself completely to the cause of women's freedom. In doing so, she risked anger, ridicule, and her career, but she emerged as one of the movement's most successful and recognizable icons and led the way to the equality girls and women enjoy and take for granted in Western society today.

While Gloria was living her successful New York life, few knew the story of the childhood she spent in poverty looking after her mentally ill mother. Gloria says her mother, Ruth Nuneviller, was once "a spirited, adventurous young woman," but she gave up the newspaper writing career she loved to help her husband, Leo Steinem, follow his dream of running a vacation resort. Leo was always chasing dreams, with little attention to matters of money or responsibility. He came from a wealthy Jewish family, while Ruth was from a modest Presbyterian background. When they married in 1921, what were called "mixed marriages" were uncommon, and some family members refused to attend the wedding. Their daughter Susanne was born in 1925. Five years later, after a stillborn baby, the death of both Ruth's and Leo's fathers, and financial troubles, Ruth had her first breakdown. She was temporarily sent to live in a home for the mentally ill.

Gloria was born four years later, on March 25, 1934. The family spent summers at the resort, and in winter, because Leo hated cold weather, they took a house trailer to California or Florida. Life on the road meant that Gloria didn't go to school for months at a time. Some years she didn't go at all.

Their lifestyle suited Leo, who was happy moving from place to place. Although her father did not provide his family with a permanent home, or have a regular job, Gloria always loved him. Later, as a writer and activist, her life was not unlike her father's: she didn't care about money and was constantly on the move. The insecure life was not good for Ruth, though, and in 1944, when Gloria was ten, her parents separated. Susanne was away at college, so Ruth and Gloria lived on their own in Toledo, Ohio, in a house Ruth's parents had left her.

This was the most difficult period of Gloria's life. Her mother became mentally ill again, was unable to sleep, and had visions of things that didn't exist. She was often confused, calling the police to report Gloria missing, because she'd forget that Gloria was in school. By Grade Six, Gloria became a mother to her own mother. Living in a rundown house in a poor neighborhood, she cared for Ruth, mostly by herself, until she was seventeen. They had little money, and Gloria remembers lying together with Ruth in bed to keep warm because the furnace didn't work. She also remembers "being bitten by one of the rats that shared our house and back alley."

Ruth finally sold the house, moved to Washington to live with Susanne, and used the house money to send Gloria to school. Gloria went to Smith College in Massachusetts, one of the largest women's colleges in the world. It was 1952.

In the 1950s, it was assumed that while women might gain a college education, after graduation their role was to get married, have children, and be good wives and mothers – not to have careers. Years later, Gloria angrily criticized colleges, including her own, for smothering "the talents and strengths of half the human race" by teaching women these values. She said female students were "brainwashed" and "every textbook told me that women didn't do anything…" But at the time, Smith gave Gloria a home free from the stress of looking after her mother, and a place to use her brain. Her studies included literature and politics, and she traveled to both Switzerland and England for school work.

In 1955, she fell in love and got engaged. It looked like she would follow the path of most female students, down the wedding aisle, but soon after she graduated in June 1956, she broke the engagement.

Gloria's many relationships with men received much attention when she became a leader of the women's movement. Feminists were often accused of being "man-haters." People believed that feminists were unhappy single women; if they just had a man they would be happy, and stop complaining. This false idea is one reason the media was fascinated with Gloria as a feminist. She didn't fit the stereotype. She had many good relationships with men and could have married, but chose not to.

Gloria traveled to India in 1957, then returned to the United States in 1958 to New York City. She began freelance writing; freelancers are paid for what they write for different publications, rather than working at just one place. Although there were few women journalists then, Gloria got good assignments. One brought her instant fame, but of a kind she would regret.

In 1963, she was asked to write an article about a Playboy Club opening in New York City. *Playboy* magazine contained photos of nude women and articles on sex. In Playboy Clubs, men were served by Playboy Bunnies –

The start of something big

The year Gloria wrote her famous Playboy Bunny story, 1963, was also the year some say second-wave feminism began, because it was when Betty Friedan's book, *The Feminine Mystique*, was published. First-wave feminism, in the 19th and 20th centuries, fought for women to be legally recognized as citizens, and for their right to vote. The second wave went much further. Friedan's book explored 1950's women and their widespread unhappiness. The causes, Friedan said, included women being forced to give up careers and only have roles as housewives and mothers. The book was an immediate bestseller and the "wave" spread to fight all forms of discrimination against women as the 60s progressed.

women dressed in skimpy costumes that showed off their legs and breasts. Gloria's assignment was to apply to work as a bunny, using a false name, and afterward, to write about it. Her article "I was a Playboy Bunny" revealed the degrading treatment and sexual comments the women constantly endured. Gloria said it was one of the "most depressing experiences in my life," but the article was a sensation. For some time after, however, magazines only wanted her to write articles with some kind of sexual element.

Despite her experience at Playboy, and her insights about the treatment of women, Gloria did not get involved in the new 1960s feminist movement until nearly the end of the decade. She was politically active in other areas. Besides protesting Vietnam, and supporting agricultural workers striking for better pay and against dangerous conditions, she supported the civil rights movement, aimed at ending discrimination against African Americans. She also worked for candidates in the Democratic Party. By 1969, she had risen up the ranks as a journalist, and had her own political opinion column, even though most political commentators were men. In March that year, she attended an event organized by a women's group, because she thought it might make a good story for her column. Instead, it changed her life.

The event was a meeting to protest American abortion laws. Abortion – the termination of pregnancy – was as controversial then as it is now. It was also illegal in most states, and because most lawmakers and politicians were male, people in the women's movement were angry. Women were the ones who got pregnant and bore children, they said, so they should have the right to choose whether to continue a pregnancy, or not. Gloria would say, "No one in their right mind is pro-abortion." But she and other feminists believed women should have the choice. In 1973, the U.S. Supreme Court agreed with them, ruling that abortion laws were unconstitutional. As a result, abortion was legalized in most cases. Before 1973, because it was against the law, some women who were desperate to end a pregnancy had abortions in situations that put their lives at risk. At the meeting, women spoke of the horror of it. Gloria was deeply moved by their stories.

The revelation that overwhelmed Gloria that day however, and changed her life, was about the ways in which men controlled almost every aspect of women's lives. She had never recognized this before, but says at the meeting she felt a "big click" about her life, and about the lives of all women – that the law and society gave men power over them, and this was wrong. She saw women as victims of discrimination, without basic rights, simply because they were born female. From that moment on, she would use all her power and talents to try and build a society that gave women more equality.

Second wave feminism was also called the Women's Liberation Movement, and it went way beyond the first-wave feminists' fight for the vote. The second wave fought for equal treatment

An ongoing debate

The 1973 Supreme Court decision, based on the famous case known as Roe v. Wade, has been challenged numerous times, but not overturned. The court cited the Constitution, which says "the government may not enter" some individual decisions, such as family planning. Many people and institutions, however, including the Roman Catholic Church and others, are profoundly opposed to abortion and say it is immoral. These groups, often called "pro-life" or "right to life," continue to work to have abortion prohibited or greatly restricted. Some politicians also argue states should once again have the right to outlaw birth control to prevent pregnancy. The Supreme Court ruled in 1965 that states did not have the authority to make contraception illegal. Before that, birth control was against the law in some states.

of women in all domains: in the home, at their jobs, in their ability to participate in everything from sports to politics. It is perhaps difficult to understand today how little equality women had back then. Employers often wouldn't hire them, and if they did, put them in the lowest jobs. Some states actually had laws limiting the hours and places women could work. Women weren't paid as well as men, and in some places they weren't allowed on juries.

In jobs women were hired for, such as flight attendants, they had to be physically attractive. They could be fired if they gained weight, and let go at age thirty-two because that was considered too old. In politics, there was one female U.S. senator at the beginning of the 1970s, and women had less than two percent of top government positions. In marriage, husbands were considered the head of the house. Sometimes women couldn't even get a credit card or a bank loan unless a man signed for them.

People were aware of the injustices of race discrimination, because of the civil rights movement, but most didn't believe discrimination against women was a problem. They just thought that was the natural way it should be. Shortly after her conversion to feminism, in April 1969, Gloria wrote a column titled "After Black Power, Women's Liberation." She compared sexism, discrimination based on gender, to discrimination based on skin color. She wrote that people believed the same untrue things about women as they did about non-whites: that black people and women had smaller brains than white men, were child-like, and couldn't look after themselves.

Male journalists warned Gloria to stay away from feminists, whom they called those "crazy women," because she'd worked so hard to build a successful career. They said being a feminist would ruin it. Overall, the media's attitude toward women's liberation was summed up by one well-known television host when he said "the whole thing" was "boring" and "ridiculous."

The media, politicians, and most of the population – including women – treated feminists as a joke and ridiculed them.

Gloria didn't care. If she was later than some coming to feminism, she made up for it with gusto and dedication. Now, it drove everything she did. But the magazines she wrote for weren't interested, so she turned to public speaking to get the message out. She had avoided this in the past because of stage fright, but it turned out she had a gift for public speaking. She was the first woman invited to speak to the National Press Club and also to first speak at the law magazine banquet at renowned Harvard University in 1971. There, she criticized members of Harvard's law school for accepting women students but still treating them as outsiders, and for allowing a professor to teach that sexual assault was a "very small" crime.

She went on speaking tours with African American women activists, including Dorothy Pitman Hughes. A photographic portrait of the two, fists raised together in the manner of the Black Power movement of the time, now hangs in the National Portrait Gallery in Washington. Gloria recognized, when some feminists didn't, that feminism often seemed directed only to white, middle-class women, and that it had to be multiracial. In 1970, she testified at government hearings for the Equal Rights Amendment – a proposed change to the American Constitution that would have prevented discrimination on the basis of sex. Gloria began appearing on the cover of *Newsweek* and many more publications. Her speaking abilities, calm manner, and "star" qualities meant the public began to take feminism more seriously. Gloria was just what the movement needed. In the roiling, boiling period of the 1960s and 70s, when it seemed almost every group in American society was rising up in revolt, women's liberation needed to get serious attention. Gloria Steinem could do that.

In 1971, Gloria, Betty Friedan, and other feminists founded the National Women's Political Caucus. The NWPC was dedicated to increasing women's presence in politics and in public offices, such as courts. That year Gloria also helped develop *Ms.* magazine, which turned out to be one of the most important tools of the women's movement. *Ms.* was the first magazine ever to be entirely created, owned, and operated by women.

Ms. began with an idea for a newsletter for a local women's group Gloria was organizing, but then it got bigger. Why not have a real magazine, run by women, with articles by women and about feminism? Until then, women's magazines were typically run by men and were mostly about things like cooking and fashion. At first Gloria didn't think it would work. Magazines make money from businesses that advertise, but many business people hated feminists. Still, the idea kept growing, and the editor of *New York Magazine*, where Gloria was a writer, was willing to publish *Ms.* as a special addition to his magazine. Gloria went ahead, despite her doubts, because "there really was nothing for women to read that was controlled by women." And women having more control was what much of feminism was about. *Ms.* was chosen as a title because the word had become a popular way to address women; like the word "Mr.," it didn't label a woman as married or unmarried, so it spoke to equality. The first edition, with Gloria as co-editor, came out Dec. 20, 1971.

Raising consciousness

Consciousness raising was a term used by 1960's feminists to describe the process of making people aware of their prejudices. These biases could be "unconscious" – people didn't realize they had them – so their understanding had to be "raised." Ideas about women's roles were what people had been taught for centuries, but that didn't make them right. Gloria said, "The first problem for all of us, men and women, is not to learn, but to unlearn." From the start, she wrote, "Women's liberation aims to free men too," because society's rules about gender roles restricted men as well.

It was a hit, selling out in just eight days, and soon *Ms.* was being published monthly. Even its founders were surprised by the response. There was a greater hunger than they had anticipated for articles about women's changing roles. They received thousands of letters applauding the publication. *Ms.* dealt with issues other magazines didn't: violence against women by their husbands, lesbians, abortion, and sexual harassment in the workplace – something that women were expected to put up with then, but that is now illegal. All this was brave and daring, but there was a price to be paid. There were vicious public attacks. One men's magazine ran a fake nude photo of Gloria with obscene comments. And Gloria was right – advertisers didn't want to put money into *Ms.* Still, the magazine survives today, and its 40th anniversary was marked with applause. Gloria continues to serve as a consulting editor.

Feminists made many gains throughout the 1970s and 1980s. Laws were enacted to prevent discrimination against women in the workplace, military academies and the armed forces were opened to women, and battered women's shelters began to appear for the first time. The first woman was appointed to the Supreme Court. Corporations began to promote women to higher positions. Attitudes and assumptions about women, that they were not as capable as men, began to change, and discrimination became less socially acceptable. There were also setbacks – especially the failure to pass the Equal Rights Amendment and make it part of the Constitution.

For Gloria, the 1980s were difficult personally. Her father had died many years earlier, alone in hospital. When her mother had a stroke, Gloria didn't want the same to happen to Ruth. Ruth died in July, 1981, with her daughters at her side. In 1986, Gloria was diagnosed with breast cancer, but she had an operation and recovered.

Then in 2000, at age sixty-six, she did something no one expected. She wed David Bale, a South African activist. Some media made fun of her, suggesting she was finally giving in, but she said she had never been against marriage, only against the marriage laws that had previously taken women's rights away. Sadly, her husband died of brain cancer less than three years after their wedding.

Setbacks

The Equal Rights Amendment was first proposed as an addition to the Constitution in 1923. It said, in part, "Equality of rights under the law shall not be denied or abridged by the United States or by any state on account of sex," It was finally approved by the Senate in 1972. But then it had to be approved by 38 state legislatures. It fell short by three states.

Today, Gloria still has a full schedule of speaking tours, writing, and activism. She is often asked whether feminism's battles aren't over and the war for equality won. To that, she answers that while women may be able to do men's work now, men still don't do what they consider women's work: especially raising children. She also points out, "I've yet to hear a man ask for advice on how to combine marriage and a career," while young women constantly ask that question. She says first-wave feminism took nearly 150 years to meet its goals. She believes society is only about twenty-five percent through the second wave, which will probably take as long.

When Gloria founded *Ms.* magazine, a famous male news anchor said, "I'll give it six months before they run out of things to say." Obviously, he was wrong. Gloria Steinem also does not run out of things to say, and she still garners media attention for feminism. *Newsweek* has called her the "enduring face of feminism for nearly half a century." The *New York Times* asked, in tribute to her, "Where is the next Gloria Steinem?"

And Oprah Winfrey, one of the world's most influential women, spoke for millions when she said, Gloria "is a trailblazer and a pioneer to me and to everybody who spells their name W-O-M-A-N. We owe her a world of gratitude for leading us to our own liberation."

JOAN BAEZ

"It is madness.
It is wrong."
1941 –

Joan Baez was only eighteen years old and suffering from horrible stage fright when she performed before an audience of 13,000 at one of America's newest music festivals. It was 1959, and a boom in the popularity of folk music meant the Newport Folk Festival "was *it*," according to one expert on the scene. Joan was almost unknown, but had been invited by a fellow artist to appear. The response was explosive. The crystal clarity of her voice and the graceful simplicity of her delivery launched her to instant fame.

The media raved. Record companies immediately tried to sign her. She went on to national tours, gold albums, and sold-out concerts, including one at Carnegie Hall, one of the most famous performance venues in the world. By 1962, she was on the cover of *Time* magazine, which described her voice as "clear as air in the autumn, a vibrant, strong, untrained and thrilling soprano." *Time* also said the twenty-one-year-old had sold more records than any other female folk singer in history.

But Joan wasn't interested in using her voice to make money. Instead, she used its spellbinding purity, and her fame, to inspire and convince audiences in the United States and around the world to join what mattered most to her: campaigns against war, racism, and injustice. She told the media who interviewed her that being called a pacifist – someone opposed to war – was more important to her than being identified as a folk singer. She spent time in jail and put her career and financial security in jeopardy because of her opposition to the American war in Vietnam. "I do not believe in war. I do not believe in the weapons of war," she wrote in a letter to the government. "Weapons and war have murdered, burned, distorted, crippled and caused endless varieties of pain...No one has the right to do that. It is madness. It is wrong."

Two important factors helped shape Joan's beliefs: religion and her Mexican heritage. Joan Chandos Baez was born January 9, 1941, on Staten Island in New York State. Her parents were Quakers, also known as the Society of Friends, and Quakers have a long tradition of pacifism. In addition, Joan had the brown skin of her Mexican father. She experienced racism as a child, and knew what it was like to be treated unfairly and as an inferior.

Both of Joan's parents were immigrants to the United States. Albert Baez moved with his family from Puebla, Mexico, when he was two. Joan's mother, born Joan Bridge, moved with her family from Scotland to the United States. Albert was a physicist and could have found a well-paid job in the defense industry, which made war weapons. As a pacifist, however, he decided he could not do defense work and became a professor instead. The family moved frequently because of his teaching at different universities. Joan, the middle of the family's three daughters, said they were "modern-day gypsies," never living in one place for longer than four years.

When they moved to California in 1951, Joan says her ethnic background was the first thing she had to deal with at junior high school. Whites and Mexicans there didn't mix, and with a Mexican name and appearance, Joan says, "Anglos couldn't accept me." But she didn't speak Spanish, so Mexicans didn't accept her either. Her sense of being different, and isolated, led her to develop her singing voice – by singing in the shower. She performed at her school's talent show, and while she didn't win the prize, she did win her classmates' respect.

As a teenager, Joan's beliefs continued to be shaped by the Quakers. She learned about Mahatma Gandhi, who had developed methods of non-violent protest in the early 1900s. And in 1956, Joan heard twenty-seven-year-old Rev. Martin Luther King, Jr. speak at a Quaker gathering about the peaceful revolution he was leading against U.S. segregation laws, which kept black people unequal. Joan says she was on her feet cheering and crying when he finished speaking. King's ideas made her think about the ways pacifists could bring change. "I knew that this was it for me." Years after this speech, Joan would join King in protest marches, and they developed and continued a relationship of mutual respect and support until he was killed by an assassin's bullet in 1968.

Joan's youth wasn't all politics and pacifism. She played guitar and had small singing engagements at high school proms and small clubs. Then, her family moved to Massachusetts. Joan started studying at Boston University, but says she lasted there only about "nine minutes," because she had the good fortune to be close to Harvard Square, one of the centers of the folk music boom. People played guitar or banjo and sang old-fashioned ballads to audiences gathered in coffee houses. Joan's career began when a friend asked her to join her in a performance. That was it. "She was just like a flower in the sunlight – when Joanie got in front of people, she bloomed," her friend said. People said she had "a voice that would make angels cry" and her stage presence was "like a beautiful bird." It didn't take long for her to receive an invitation to Newport. After that, Joan says, "I was the 'folk queen,' bingo, just like that."

Joan began using her clout as a celebrity to help the civil rights cause. Segregation policies kept blacks and whites separate in Southern states, in everything from schools to bathrooms. In August 1963, seven years after first meeting King, she took part in the March on Washington for Jobs and Freedom for African Americans. It was one of the largest-ever political rallies for human rights in U.S. history; about a quarter of a million people took part. King gave his famous "I Have a Dream" speech, calling for an end to racism in America. Joan led the crowds in singing "We Shall Overcome," which had become the anthem of the civil rights movement. It celebrated the certainty that some day the struggle would be over, and the goals of peace and equality achieved.

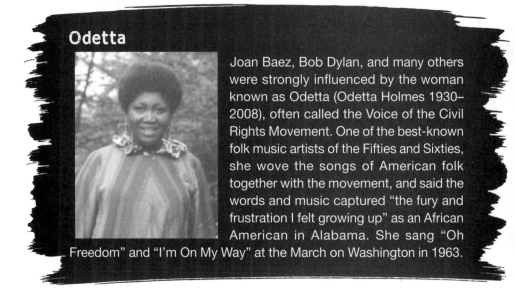

Odetta

Joan Baez, Bob Dylan, and many others were strongly influenced by the woman known as Odetta (Odetta Holmes 1930–2008), often called the Voice of the Civil Rights Movement. One of the best-known folk music artists of the Fifties and Sixties, she wove the songs of American folk together with the movement, and said the words and music captured "the fury and frustration I felt growing up" as an African American in Alabama. She sang "Oh Freedom" and "I'm On My Way" at the March on Washington in 1963.

Although Joan took part in political events, most of the songs she sang weren't political – yet. They were still traditional folk ballads. Joan described them as being about "love and death and beauty." But that day in Washington, Joan sang with a lesser-known folk singer. Bob Dylan was to become one of America's most celebrated singer-songwriters, a mythic figure and a legend to many. It was Joan, at the top of the folk music scene, who helped boost his career. But Dylan also helped change hers.

When Joan first heard him sing protest songs he had written about the looming disaster of nuclear weapons, about the arms race between America and Russia, and about the cruel injustice of America's racism, she was "bowled over" and "knocked out." She realized these types of songs could bring her music and her pacifist and political beliefs together. She was getting tired of what she had been singing, and it was clear to her, "this was the direction to go." From now on, she would sing her politics.

Joan's first recordings of Dylan's songs in 1963 included "With God on Our Side," a song that ridiculed those who waged war believing God supported their killing and destruction. She also performed Dylan's "Blowin' in the Wind," which became an anti-war classic. "The Times They Are A-Changin'" challenged the ways that politicians and the older generation ran things. Joan sang it at a gala dinner for the new President, Lyndon B. Johnson, right after she told the audience America should not be part of the war in Vietnam. Dylan's music – performed by Joan, by Dylan, and by Joan and Dylan together – gripped the imagination of a generation about to be sent off to war.

Vietnam, in Southeast Asia, was a country divided: North Vietnam was communist. South Vietnam, a U.S. ally, was not. North Vietnam wanted to take over the whole country and make it communist, and so the United States got increasingly involved in the conflict on the side of the South. By 1963, there were 16,000 American troops in the country, and in 1964, America began bombing North Vietnam. Joan didn't believe in war – and she certainly didn't believe in *this* war. At that time, however, most Americans supported U.S. soldiers being in Vietnam. Joan wanted to change that, and stop the killing. Using her music, her fame, and the protest methods she learned as a teenager, she began the biggest non-violent campaign of her life. It was to last a decade.

Some of Joan's anti-war work involved civil disobedience that broke the law. In 1964, after the American bombing started, she wrote a letter to the government telling them she had calculated the amount of her taxes that would be used to finance the war, and she would not pay that portion. That action helped launch a national movement of people withholding taxes, many of them celebrities like Joan. Some sources say war tax resistance, which had been used previously in the United States as a form of protest, gained its greatest strength ever during the Vietnam War period. It brought attention to the cause, but there were consequences for Joan.

The government took her to court, and she was attacked publicly for her views. Some people considered war protesters

Protest songs

There is a long history of music sung for political causes. The 1960s came to be defined as an era of protest, and music has a prominent place in that history. The anti-war cause was especially associated with protest songs, and the music of Joan Baez and Bob Dylan led the way. Music can't stop a war, of course, but it can inspire and unite people in a cause. By 1965 Dylan was moving away from politics and protest. His and Joan's relationship, which was both romantic and professional, fell apart. Joan was disappointed by the change in Dylan, but later paid him tribute, saying his songs were "the most powerful stuff we had" in the non-violent campaign.

traitors, and she was not allowed to give a concert at Constitution Hall in Washington D.C. because of her activities. Joan responded by giving a free concert at the Washington Monument instead; about 30,000 people attended. It was one of many concerts she performed in the Sixties, where she rallied the crowds singing protest songs.

The anti-war movement was small when Joan took her strong stand in 1964, but it began to grow through the last half of the decade as more groups began to organize themselves. Some were student groups. Others, such as Women Strike for Peace, were led by concerned mothers and female politicians. Leaders of the civil rights movement got involved. People staged mass demonstrations and marches. Young men publicly burned their draft cards to protest being drafted into the military to be sent to Vietnam to fight.

Joan took part in many of these actions, and also tried to persuade men who had been drafted not to go to Vietnam. She visited army centers where draftees were being shipped out and ask them to become draft resisters or "draft dodgers" – the term for those who fled to Canada or went into hiding to escape military service. She sometimes succeeded in changing a draftee's mind, although resisting draft orders was against the law. But more often, she would be jeered, spit at, and kicked.

In 1967, she and at least forty others were arrested for taking part in a sit-in protest at a military center. Joan spent ten days in prison that time, and would be imprisoned again for similar actions. But she said these experiences only made her a stronger pacifist, and it was vital that her anti-war work include more than singing. "If you're committed to singing meaningful songs, you also have to be committed to leading a life that backs that up." A fellow musician said no matter what she was subjected to, "She'd go right back and start over. That's a kind of courage you don't see often."

In 1968, Joan married fellow activist David Harris, who had visited her in prison. The following year he was taken to prison himself for refusing to serve in the military. Joan was pregnant; she and David would have a son, Gabriel, but would divorce after a few years. At the time, however, neither her husband's imprisonment nor pregnancy curtailed her anti-war activities. That same year, 1969, there was an event some consider the peak of music protests and events of the era. It was called Woodstock.

The Woodstock Music and Arts Fair began on a farm in upper New York State on August 15, billed as "three days of peace and music." Some estimates say 400,000 people came to hear a wide variety of famous musicians perform. They included Janis Joplin, The Who, Jimi Hendrix, and Joan Baez. Joan led the crowd in anti-war songs and closed the first day's performances. In the anti-Vietnam war atmosphere that dominated Woodstock, she was said to be a perfect choice.

By 1971, more Americans agreed with what Joan had said from the beginning: they should get out of Vietnam. Public support for the war had steadily declined. In 1965, opinion polls showed 61 percent of Americans supported it. By 1971, that number had dropped to 28 percent. There were many reasons Americans lost their taste

The cost of Vietnam

About 300,000 U.S. soldiers were wounded and more than 58,000 Americans were killed or went missing in Vietnam. The Vietnam Veterans Memorial in Washington honors all those who were lost, with a long wall inscribed with their names. As many as one and a quarter million North and South Vietnamese soldiers are estimated to have died by the time the war ended in 1975. The number of Vietnamese civilians who died during the U.S. part of the war is not accurately known; there are estimates of between one and three million people.

for the conflict half a world away. It was killing their young men. They saw the horror of it in the media. And they were sickened by reports of the American role in massacring peaceful Vietnamese villagers in places such as My Lai. Joan Baez, other leading anti-war figures, and peace organizations had also certainly had an impact by increasing awareness and uniting anti-war opinion.

Despite the drop in public support, in 1972 the United States was still in the war. That was the year Joan, as a war resister, endured the greatest risk to her life. She went to North Vietnam in December and visited the capital, Hanoi, as part of a peace group. Hanoi had not been bombed by the Americans for some time, but while Joan was there, the so-called "Christmas bombing" began. It was the most intense of the whole Vietnamese war. Joan was terrified as she saw others killed, but eventually returned home safely. Within one month of this visit, a peace agreement was signed, and within three months, by March 29, 1973, the last American military units left Vietnam. Her non-violent war against America's involvement in the war was over.

It's been about four decades since the conflict fully ended, with the North Vietnamese taking over the country in 1975.

At risk to herself

Joan took physical risks many times in her protest work. During civil rights marches in the South, she walked with black children who were being attacked by people throwing bricks and rocks because African Americans were finally allowed to attend white-only schools. Joan hoped her presence as a celebrity, being followed by TV news cameras, would deter the violence. Civil rights activist Jesse Jackson said, "In that setting, which was hostile and dangerous, there was Joan Baez." Most artists, he adds, protected their careers by drawing away from the civil rights struggle. "She came."

In those decades, Joan Baez never stopped singing, never stopped working for the cause of non-violence, and never stopped visiting other war zones. She has also opposed the death penalty for prisoners, supported gay and lesbian rights, and has taken action against poverty. The span of her work has resulted in a wide range of awards and honors – from the Thomas Merton Award in 1975 – named for the well-known American priest, and given annually to those who struggle for justice – to an award named for Joan herself by Amnesty International in 2011. Amnesty International is a global human rights organization that won the Nobel Peace Prize in 1977.

For her part, Joan says she is happiest and healthiest when she's wrapped up in political causes. In the year she turned seventy, she was on the streets of New York City, singing for the crowds of the Occupy Wall Street movement, which was protesting against big banks and large multinational corporations, and the increasing poverty of the many compared to the extreme wealth of the few. She has spent her life the way she wanted to – singing – and calls the songs she chose to sing her "best friends." They are "connected to peoples' lives and suffering and real issues," she says. "There's no music for me outside of that."

LEILANI MUIR

"Nobody has the right to play God with other people's lives — nobody."

1944 –

When Leilani Muir's mother put her in an institution in 1955, Leilani was just a few days away from her eleventh birthday. She had no idea she was being abandoned by her family and didn't realize there was anything different about the place where she was left. She only thought the other children there were like her: "nobody wanted them."

But the institution in the Canadian province of Alberta existed for a special reason. The Provincial Training School for Mental Defectives housed children who supposedly had mental disabilities. "Mental defective" or "feeble-minded" were some of the terms used then. Ten years later, Leilani left the school and discovered what they had done to her without her knowledge. At age fourteen she was "sterilized"– she underwent an operation that removed her fallopian tubes. She would never be able to have children.

What happened to Leilani happened to thousands of others in Canada, and hundreds of thousands around the world. It was the result of a belief in eugenics. Eugenics supporters believed people with mental disabilities were criminal and immoral, and a threat to society. They believed such people should be confined in institutions so they didn't mix with "normal" people, and that they should be prevented from having children. Otherwise, their "defects" would be passed on, and that would weaken society overall. So-called "scientific tests" were used to determine who was mentally "unfit." The science and methods of eugenics have now been completely discredited. The tests were wrong. Many people who were normal mentally were labeled "feeble-minded," including Leilani Muir.

Nearly forty years after her operation, Leilani fought back. She became the first person to take the provincial government to court over what was done. She did it because she wanted the public to know the cruelty that had been carried out in the name of science and to prevent it ever happening again.

Leilani was born in Calgary, Alberta, on July 15, 1944. Her twenty-year-old mother was married for the second time to a man named Earl Draycott.

What is eugenics?

Eugenics means "well-born" in Greek. In the early 20th century, the eugenics movement promoted the idea that human beings could be scientifically bred for improvement in the same way farm animals are bred. Its supporters said only people with desirable traits should be allowed to reproduce and have children. Weaker people with less desirable traits should not. But who had the power to make the decisions about who was desirable? Often the decisions were based on racist ideas about what groups were "weak" and undesirable.

He was away in military service when Leilani was born, and it's uncertain who her real father was. Her mother, referred to in Leilani's court case only as Ms. Scorah, was living at the time with a man named H. G. Scorah. She had been born in Poland, was Roman Catholic, and had first been married at age fourteen. Including Leilani, she gave birth to four children in just six years.

The Scorahs were poor and moved around a lot. They lived on an isolated farm far from neighbors, which Leilani says made it easier for her mother to abuse her. She says her mother beat her and didn't feed her, so because she was starving, she stole lunches from other children at school. This led to the family being referred to a clinic with a doctor, psychologist, and social worker when Leilani was seven years old. Besides stealing lunches, there is no record from this clinic of Leilani having any other problems or mental disabilities. The records do show, however, that her mother admitted to having a drinking problem.

Leilani says her mother told her she had never wanted to have girls, and that's why she didn't want to keep Leilani. In 1952, when she was only eight, Leilani was placed in a convent for a month. Then, on July 12, 1955, her mother took her to the Provincial Training School in Red Deer, Alberta, and signed forms to have her admitted. The school had opened five years before the Alberta Sexual Sterilization Act was passed in 1928 as a result of the eugenics craze. The province of British Columbia also passed sterilization laws, but Alberta's was the most comprehensive and had the biggest impact.

The idea of eugenics began in the late 1800s. By the 1900s it was having an impact worldwide, and its growth was fuelled by racism. There was widespread concern that society was being weakened by an overall decline in intelligence. Some of this was blamed on increases in the number of immigrants and non-white people. They became frequent targets of forced sterilization because they were considered mentally inferior, and people thought if they were allowed to have children their numbers would increase and society would go downhill. White Protestant people of British origin were the favored group in Canada, while East Europeans and Aboriginal people, including Métis, were most often singled out for the operations. In total, nearly 3,000 people were forcibly sterilized in Alberta. Of these, 25 percent were Aboriginal, even though they made up less than four percent of the population.

Leilani would have been considered a member of an inferior group because her mother was an Eastern European Catholic. Still, Leilani was not tested to see if she actually was mentally disabled when she was first admitted to the Red Deer school. Her mother signed some admission forms, and officials accepted them. They ignored a doctor's report stating that Leilani might have emotional problems, but not a "mental deficiency." In the institution, she received some lower grade levels of education and got good reports. She was also provided with a few advantages over her home life. Leilani said there were "toys to play with, a clean bed, clean clothes

Who else did it?

Several U.S. states and countries such as Sweden, Austria, Switzerland, Belgium, and the Czech Republic all practiced forced sterilization. The eugenics movement also became popular in Germany in the 1920s and 1930s. Sterilization was seen as a way to develop racial purity and superiority, a concept of ultimate importance to Nazi leader Adolph Hitler. The Nazis are estimated to have sterilized 300,00 to 400,000 people. Nazi race policies led to the murder of six million Jews and millions of others belonging to groups considered undesirable or inferior, such as the handicapped. After the Nazi horrors, many North American jurisdictions repealed their sterilization laws. Alberta and British Columbia did not repeal theirs until the 1970s.

and three meals a day," and the other girls there were "like sisters." Her mother had so little contact with her daughter that a school administrator wrote to her after Leilani had been at Red Deer nearly a year. The administrator said, "She is beginning to feel you have forgotten her." After this, Leilani did have more contact with her family and sometimes went home to visit.

In November 1957, more than two years after she arrived at Red Deer, Leilani was given an I.Q. test to measure her intelligence. Today we know that I.Q. tests were poorly designed and inaccurate. There were many factors that could lead to a low score, even if you had normal intelligence. The test questions were more easily understood if you were white, middle-class, and an English-speaking North American. But if you were an immigrant whose English was not good, or from a different culture, or were poor and had limited experience of North America, you wouldn't do as well. Those like Leilani, who had been abused, had emotional difficulties, and whose education was designed for less-capable children, had additional risks of having low scores.

I.Q. tests put people in different categories, and Leilani's test said she was below normal, a "mental-defective moron." Being placed in this category meant that she could be sterilized. Leilani's records from

The bias of intelligence tests

In one study done in the spring of 1913, intelligence tests given to immigrants entering the United States showed over 80 percent were "feeble-minded." This was obviously not true, but the scientist who published the research believed it was, as did many others. They believed it because their ideas of immigrants were racist, and because their belief in "science" was so strong, they didn't understand that their own biases were creating these results.

this time say her "mental deficiency" could be passed on if she had children and that she was "incapable of intelligent parenthood." So on January 18, 1959, when she was just fourteen, Leilani was taken to a room and told she would have her appendix out. Then she was given the surgery that also sterilized her.

Court documents show this was just shortly after she had started her period. The fact that she was menstruating is important because it shows that Leilani was then physically capable of becoming pregnant. And pregnancy was exactly what the government's Eugenics Board, which worked closely with the school, wanted to prevent. In later years, it was revealed that residents of the school were the largest single group in Alberta to be sterilized without their knowledge or permission.

In 1965, after ten years at the training school, Leilani decided to leave. She was nearly twenty-one years old but says she only had a Grade Five education and was poorly prepared for life. She married the first man she dated. When she went to a doctor to find out why she wasn't getting pregnant, tests revealed the reason. She says for years she couldn't accept the truth and kept searching for ways to repair the damage. It couldn't be done. Leilani remembers being told "my insides looked like I'd been through a slaughterhouse," by one doctor. "Those were his exact words." Her first marriage ended in divorce, and she says her inability to have children was a major reason her second marriage also ended.

The emotional devastation of not being able to have children meant visits to a psychiatrist. The psychiatrist she saw in 1975 said her emotional state was "understandable...the damage done to her self image and to her reproductive capacity cannot be undone."

By 1989, living in Victoria, British Columbia, Leilani says she almost reached a point of no return. She was considering suicide. She believes her faith led her to a mental-health group that helped her. In the process of determining what kind of treatment she should have, she was given another intelligence test. The results astounded the doctors. They showed Leilani's intelligence was normal. Leilani was not, as she had been labeled in 1957, a "moron."

Given all that had happened to her – being wrongly labeled mentally defective and sterilized without her knowledge or consent – Leilani's doctors told her she should sue the government. Leilani agreed it was time the province of Alberta admitted its mistakes. Its sterilization law had been repealed in 1972, forty-four years after it was first passed. But the public was completely unaware of its victims.

Leilani approached a law firm and asked them to take her case against the province. One other woman did the same, but eventually settled out of court and was barred from talking about it. What the province had done had received no public attention. Leilani's case would be public, and that's what Leilani wanted. She wanted people to know exactly what had happened.

The legal papers were filed in 1989, but the trial did not begin until June 1995. It received huge attention as the first case of its kind to go to court in Canada. Leilani says about one hundred media people were waiting for her on that first day, and it "scared the living life out of me." By now she was fifty years old, working part-time in a cafeteria in Victoria, lived independently and went to church occasionally. She gardened and enjoyed needlework and reading. Suddenly, she was the subject of television reports and newspaper headlines all across Canada.

Over the next several weeks she told the court the painful story of her past. Her parents were both dead by this time, and lawyers for the government tried to cast doubt on some of her family history, including whether she had really been abused by her mother. The government admitted she should not have been sterilized, but said it hadn't broken any human rights laws, because none existed at the time in either Canada or Alberta.

Trial witnesses included a former member of the Eugenics Board, which had approved sterilizations. The court was horrified to learn from her testimony that boys with Down syndrome, a condition that delays mental development, were also sterilized, even though that Down syndrome males were unable to father children. Sterilization was unnecessary.

Leilani's lawsuit sought compensation from the province, not just for being sterilized but also for being classified as a moron, and for being held in an institution for ten years without having been properly tested. At one point during the trial, the government offered to pay her $60,000 plus interest on that amount from the time she began the legal action. Leilani was insulted that what she had endured should be considered of such little worth. "God made me a whole person," she says, and "when they sterilized me, they made me half a person." Alberta's offer was "a slap in the face."

When the judge made her ruling on January 25, 1996, she awarded Leilani Muir almost $750,000.

Surprising eugenics supporters

Some of Canada's best-known human rights activists and progressive politicians supported eugenics at the height of its popularity. They include the women known as The Famous Five: feminists who led the fight for women to be recognized legally as persons in Canada. They, too, considered mentally disabled people a threat. Tommy Douglas, a Baptist minister turned politician – who is revered for his leadership in enacting important Canadian policies, such as free medical care – was also an early supporter of eugenics. He changed his mind, however, after seeing what was happening in Germany when he visited there in 1936. Later, as Saskatchewan's Minister of Health, he passionately rejected forced sterilization.

It was the maximum amount allowed by law for pain and suffering. Justice Joanne Veit's explanation of her decision was blunt. She said the hurt Leilani experienced as a result of her sterilization "will continue far into the future." She said she was convinced the emotional and physical damage was "catastrophic," and she described the circumstances of Leilani's sterilization as "high-handed" and "contemptuous" on the part of officials. She said there was so little respect for Leilani's human dignity that "the community's and the court's sense of decency is offended." She also awarded extra money for damages because Leilani's stay at the school had deprived her of the opportunity for normal development.

Leilani speaks publicly about her life so that others will never share the same fate.

Justice Veit did not confine her conclusions to Leilani's case. She also said the way doctors at the Eugenics Board and others had treated the Down syndrome boys was "repugnant" and sickening. As for those who were sterilized, she said it was obvious much of the early eugenics movement in Canada was racist. She said it was based on concerns held by those of British stock about "the potential weakening of the race by immigrants," which they wanted to prevent by controlling the reproduction of those they regarded as inferior.

Leilani won a victory not just for herself, but also for the government's other victims. After she went to court, at least seven hundred others followed her lead and sued the province. The media expressed its disgust for what the public now knew; newspapers said Alberta's provincial government had carried out "one of the worst human rights violations in Canadian history." They called Leilani a hero. One columnist said, "Let us acknowledge her bravery, and...her fine intelligence" and concluded Leilani "deserves every penny."

Others wrote that the eugenics program had been dangerous and wrong, and that "it sounds a warning bell for the future." Since the ability to test people for possible genetic weaknesses is rapidly advancing, they wondered if eugenics ideas could return.

Leilani was happy that other victims benefitted from what she had done, but said the money she and others received did not take the hurt away, because the government "took something very precious away from all of us." But she also said all the attention the case received means, "we can make sure it doesn't happen again." Today, Leilani continues to make public appearances, in media and at conferences, to ensure this dark time in Canadian history and the whole story of eugenics is not forgotten. "Nobody," she says, "has the right to play God with other people's lives – nobody."

TEMPLE GRANDIN

"We've got to give
animals a decent life."

1947 –

Temple Grandin discovered her life's purpose when she was
in her twenties. She wanted to stop the pain and suffering
of animals. Not wild animals, or exotic, rare animals, or even
pets, but farm animals such as cows, pigs, and chickens. We
eat them, but rarely think about them.

Temple witnessed the cruelty inflicted on these creatures
when she was studying cattle and the meat industry in university. People in the business thought livestock were just
"things" – products to be sold for profit. They didn't think of
the animals as fellow living beings. The creatures were often
subjected to grotesque, torturous conditions while alive, and
suffered needlessly at their deaths. That's what Temple was
determined to change.

Women and animals

Women have taken the lead in animal rights and welfare movements in the United States and Great Britain since the 1800s. They include Frances Power Cobbe, who in 1875 founded the first organization protesting the use of animals in experiments. It is called the National Anti-Vivisection Society. Cobbe was also a leader in the fight for votes for women. The woman who praised Temple Grandin for so profoundly reducing suffering was Ingrid Newkirk, who co-founded PETA in 1980.

Today, humane treatment of livestock has vastly improved, largely due to Temple Grandin. Her impact has been so astonishing that the president of one of the foremost animal rights organizations, People for the Ethical Treatment of Animals (PETA), says Temple "has done more to reduce suffering in the world than any other person...." PETA and countless other national and international organizations, from animal welfare groups and humane societies to the meat industry itself, have recognized her achievements with special awards and honors. *Time* magazine named her one of the world's most influential people and a hero. This is all the more remarkable because when Temple was only three years old, she was diagnosed with the brain disorder called autism.

Temple was born on August 29, 1947, in Boston, Massachusetts, the first of four children of Eustacia and Dick Grandin. Eustacia noticed her baby's behavior was different from others, but blamed it on her own inexperience as a mother. By the time Temple was two-and-a-half, her problems were increasingly obvious. She wasn't talking or laughing and had violent temper tantrums. She wouldn't respond when spoken to, as if she were deaf, yet loud noises terrified her. These are common behaviors of autistic children, but in the late 1940s, autism had only recently been recognized as a condition. Her father said Temple was mentally retarded and accused his wife of ignoring the obvious. At age three, tests showed no signs of retardation, but shortly after a psychiatrist diagnosed her as autistic.

Little about autism was understood then and there are still many mysteries about it, including its cause, although estimates say one in eighty-eight children may have an autism disorder. It affects people in different ways. Some, like Temple as a young child, don't speak, while their senses, such as hearing and smell, may be exaggerated. Temple says her ears are like microphones, so normal noise can be incredibly painful. Often autistic people don't like being touched, won't make eye contact, and find it difficult to be with others. They will sometimes spin endlessly in circles, repeat the same words over and over, or stare at one object for a long time.

Temple had many of these behaviors. When she got older and spoke publicly about being autistic, she said the strongest emotions she felt when she was young were fear and anxiety, and spinning somehow helped relieve that. She also said that autism was like a prison. "It was as if a sliding glass door separated me from the world of love and human understanding."

After Temple was diagnosed, her father insisted she be put in an institution. Eustacia was dead set against it. Instead, she hired a special nanny and a speech therapist to work with Temple. Eventually her daughter began to talk, and when Temple was five, Eustacia found a private school for her. It was for "normal" children, but had small classes and was close to their home. Despite her problems, Temple did well there. She still had terrible temper tantrums and odd behaviors, but was good in art and at building things. Her classmates were mostly kind to her, and she made some friends. One said, "I like her because she's not boring."

Temple didn't understand that she was different from other people and wouldn't fully realize this for many years.

She thought it was *other* children who were different. In high school, she ran into problems. There were hundreds of students, and each class had a different teacher. This was a lot of change for someone with autism, because change often causes anxiety and fear. Other students were mean to her, calling her "tape recorder" because she repeated stories again and again, using exactly the same phrases each time. They called her "weirdo" and "dummy." One girl spat out at her, "You're nothing but a retard!" Anger ripped through Temple, and she threw a book at the girl, hitting her in the eye. Temple was expelled.

This turned out to be a gift. Temple's mother researched schools for children with problems like her daughter's, and in January 1960, Temple went to live at the Mountain Country School in Vermont. There, she began to discover a special interest in animals. The school had horses, and Temple loved them so much that when the teachers needed to discipline her for bad behavior, they took away her animal privileges.

Most importantly, this school is where Temple met the teacher she calls her "salvation" – William Carlock. He knew how to draw out the best in Temple because he didn't try to force her to be "normal." He tried to understand how her mind worked and how she saw the world. He also assured her she was a gifted and worthwhile person. Before Temple met Mr. Carlock, she didn't work hard at school and mostly didn't do very well. "Because of him and other dedicated teachers and Mother's faith in me," she says, "I began to study."

By this time, Temple's mother had divorced and remarried. Temple now had a new aunt, Ann Brecheen, who had a cattle ranch in Arizona, and Eustacia thought it would be good for Temple to spend a summer there. But any new experience still created overwhelming anxiety. Despite the improvements at her school, Temple's teenage years were some of the worst for anxiety attacks. She longed for relief, feeling trapped by her distress.

Physical work at the ranch helped somewhat. But what Temple had always longed for, and yet could not physically tolerate, was to be held. Hugs made her feel suffocated and afraid, even though she craved them. Since she was five years old, Temple had dreamed of making a machine that could hold and comfort her. Machines didn't frighten her the way people did. That summer, animals helped her find what she was searching for.

Cattle ranchers use a device called a squeeze chute – a wood and metal cage that holds a cow still while it's getting a needle or being branded. Temple noticed that when the cows first went into the machine, they were frightened and anxious. But when the sides of the cage moved in to "squeeze" the animal, the result was astonishing. The cow was completely calmed. Temple thought it might calm her as well. Perhaps this was the machine she had always imagined!

She convinced her aunt to let her go inside and to move the sides in to "hold" her, just as she would with a cow. Temple was right. The machine relaxed her – like a massage.

When she returned to school that fall, Mr. Carlock encouraged her to design and build her own human squeeze machine, and she did. Her psychiatrist thought she shouldn't use it, that it was "sick." Even her mother, who almost always supported Temple, didn't think the machine was a good idea. But it helped Temple's anxiety attacks, and she continued to build better and better versions of it. Her squeeze machine also motivated Temple to get an education. She wanted to understand exactly why it worked. For "the first time in my life," she said, "I felt a purpose for learning."

Temple graduated from high school second in her class in 1966 and went on to study at Franklin Pierce College, where she earned a degree in psychology in 1970.

Graduate school was next. She studied for a Master of Science degree, specializing in animal behavior at Arizona

State University. In yet another new place, all the old feelings of fear, anxiety, and worthlessness returned. But Temple was about to experience the special insight that would lead to her life's calling.

Part of her university research involved observing cattle at a feedlot, where they are fed, vaccinated, and made ready for market. There, they had to be moved through long narrow passageways, or chutes. Sometimes – for no apparent reason – they would suddenly get frightened in the chute and stop moving. Nobody knew why. To get them moving again, workers prodded the animals with painful electric shocks, panicking them even more. Owners didn't care about the animals' welfare. Their concern was simply that production slowed down when the cattle reacted this way. Slowdowns meant lost money.

Temple went inside the chute herself to look at it from the cattle's point of view and get inside their heads. What was spooking them? The people at the feed yards thought she was ridiculous. Cows, to them, were just something to sell. They didn't consider that the animals might have thoughts. But Temple did.

Taking pride in difference

When Temple was suffering so badly from anxiety at Arizona State, her mother wrote her this: "Be proud you are different. All bright people who have contributed to life have been different and found the path of life lonely. While the joiners and social butterflies flutter about, Temple, you'll get real things done." Temple followed her mother's advice. One of Temple's many famous quotes is, "I am different, not less." She advocates for people with autism, in addition to her animal work, writing books, and speaking publicly. She also has a website that helps autistic people and their families. The "squeeze machine" Temple developed all those years ago has also been used to help autistic children.

That's what her research was about: how animals perceive and think about the world. She concluded that animals must think in pictures, not words, because they don't have words. Her bigger discovery, however, was about herself. She realized she thought the same way the cattle did!

As Temple explains it, "I have no words in my head at all, just pictures." If someone says the word "dog" or "shoe," she sees it in her head as if she were looking at a detailed photograph. She didn't know for years that this is not the way most people think. Now, Temple understood that her autism meant her thinking, in this respect, was like animal thinking. She also believes the way she experiences the world – seeing a lot of details all together, rather than just one thing, and having highly developed senses of smell and hearing – is similar to an animal's experience.

Thinking the way an animal did made Temple valuable to the meat industry because she could "translate" animal behavior, as if she spoke their language. When she went inside that cattle chute, she saw it the way a cow would and understood what scared them. A clanking chain hanging down, or deep shadows, would make them balk. She discovered cows were afraid of the color yellow, or a coat flapping in the wind. Now, meat industry owners didn't think she was so crazy. If an animal was upset, it

Thinking in pictures

Temple's book *Thinking in Pictures* explains how she experiences the world as an autistic person. An award-winning movie biography entitled *Temple Grandin* also illustrates this aspect of her life and a British television documentary about her is called *The Woman Who Thinks Like a Cow*. Many of Temple's other books about animal thinking and behavior have been bestsellers. These include *Animals in Translation* and *Animals Make Us Human*. They portray animals as thinking and feeling beings.

might injure itself, and bruised meat can't be used for human food. Stressed pigs have lower quality meat, and a stressed dairy cow gives less milk. Temple was helping their businesses by protecting their "products."

These attitudes toward animals – seeing them as "things" – weren't confined to industry. When Temple began her college studies, many animal scientists didn't believe animals had emotions or intelligence. Temple came to believe differently. Working with cattle, she developed a closeness and respect for them. She tuned into the way cows suffered from the same emotions of fear and anxiety that she did, because of how they were handled and treated. She also witnessed people being cruel. Besides electric shocks, they would beat the animals or do other vicious things. They seemed to think it didn't matter because the animals were just going to die and become food anyway.

As Temple's own awareness about cattle increased, she saw this was wrong and wrote in her diary, "My answer to this is: what if your grandmother was in the hospital dying? How would you like it if the doctor said, 'She's just a terminal patient. We can throw her over in a corner.'" Watching animals be killed, she says, made her think more about death and God, and she says she came to realize each animal was "an individual, and God's creation," just like people. This was a turning point. She decided this meant they should be treated well when they are alive and die without suffering. "Nature is cruel," she says, "but we don't have to be." Once she saw livestock as fellow creatures, she dedicated her life to improving theirs.

Temple started her revolution in animal welfare by combining the creative and building skills she'd had since grade school with her unique ability to think like an animal. She designed machines and systems that would lessen animals' fears and anxieties.

The same year she received her master's degree, 1975, she founded her own company, Grandin Livestock Handling Systems Inc. Her first breakthrough was a new system for immersing cattle in deep pools to treat them for parasites and disease. The structure in use at the time forced cattle to go down a slide to get into the water. It frightened them, and they would sometimes flip over into the pool and drown. Temple's system got rid of the slide and let the cattle step in calmly. Her design drew national and international attention from ranchers, and her reputation grew.

Then, she came up with another revolutionary idea for cattle chutes, based on her understanding of how cows think and act. The chutes used then ran in straight lines, and cattle were supposed to walk through them. Temple understood cows are most comfortable walking on a curved path, so she made her chutes circular, which kept the animals more peaceful.

Some people in the meat business remained doubtful, until they saw how well Temple's ideas worked. But doubt was not the only obstacle she faced. Temple was a woman working in an almost entirely male world, and many men didn't want her around, or were jealous of her success. One time at a feedlot, men covered her car with bloody animal parts. Another time, managers at a meat processing plant took her on a tour and three times returned to the same place: the blood pits where bodies are hung for the blood to drain out. Why three times? "They just wanted to make me throw up," she says. "They wanted to gross me out."

But the use of Temple's equipment and methods spread. She continued to devise new ways to work with livestock, and all her inventions were praised for reducing animals' suffering by reducing their fear. Today, at least half the cattle in the United States and Canada are handled in humane systems Temple designed, and a large proportion of hogs are as well. Many other countries outside North America also use her systems. That's just one reason animal activists praise her for the great change she has achieved.

Temple moved to Fort Collins to teach at Colorado State University in 1990, the year after she earned her PhD. In that decade, her impact on humane handling methods for animals became enormous, as the fast food industry began to turn to her for help. There are approximately ten billion food animals in the United States alone, and many of them are used in fast food – everything from hamburgers to fried chicken. In 1997 a judgment in a lawsuit involving McDonald's found the company responsible for cruelty to some animals.

Alarmed at what this would do to its business, McDonald's hired Temple to review its animal practices. She took company executives to a slaughterhouse, and they were shocked by what they saw. After that, Temple says, "they were like, 'Ye gads, we've got to make some changes." As a result, McDonald's says it was the first major company to demand that its suppliers treat animals humanely.

That spurred other companies to do the same. Temple began advising large restaurant chains, including Wendy's and Burger King. Dozens of large corporations that provide

Temple on being vegetarian

Given how close Temple feels to animals, and what she has seen in the meat industry, some might expect her to be vegetarian. She isn't. She has a condition called Ménière's disease and says not eating meat made her feel dizzy. Still, "If I had my druthers," she says, "people would have evolved as plant-eaters and wouldn't kill animals for food at all." But she doesn't see the majority of people changing their meat-eating habits soon, and so she says the most important thing she can do to help animals is to ensure feedlots and slaughterhouses are humanely run. "We've got to give animals a decent life." According to Temple, "It really is possible to care deeply about animals and eat meat."

Temple Grandin makes a point during a 2010 TED lecture.

most of the meat, eggs, and milk in North America also asked Temple how to improve conditions for livestock. She began to write rules and guidelines for the American Meat Institute, the nation's oldest and largest meat and poultry trade association. None had existed before. Temple also created a system to measure whether meat processing companies meet the U.S. government guidelines, laid out in the Humane Slaughter Act. Some of the cruel practices Temple has tried to eliminate include hanging cows or chickens upside down by one leg, causing them to scream in pain and terror before they are killed with a sharp knife.

Temple says cows have become the best treated of all farm animals, but there is still much to be done about pigs and chickens. She is working to stop the practice of raising chickens and pigs in cages so small the animals can't even stand up or turn around. She has seen chickens packed so tightly on top of each other that they have lost their feathers from rubbing and stress. Egg-laying chickens sometimes have their beaks cut in order to stop them pecking. She has seen workers load chickens by holding one wing, which snaps the bones in half. She constantly seeks meetings with farmers or management heads in corporations to try and convince them to change their methods.

"Animals," Temple says, "have special talents normal people don't," and autistic people do as well. But the genius of both is invisible to most of us. She wants people to change the way they think about animals and autistic people. Temple says even if she could somehow snap her fingers and no longer be autistic, she wouldn't do it. She travels all over North America appearing at conferences and in the media to spread her message. Perhaps the most important is the one she directs to young people: "The true meaning of life," she says, "is if you do something that makes real change. That's what matters."

MICHELLE DOUGLAS

"I couldn't believe I could be fired on that basis."

1963 –

Michelle Douglas wanted to spend her life helping others. As a young woman, she decided the best way to do that was to join Canada's military; she believed serving in the armed forces was noble work. Once she signed up, Michelle's military bosses quickly identified her as a star with an outstanding career ahead of her. She finished top of her class in both basic and security-officer training. One colonel ranked her in the top five percent of all the officers he had worked with in his nearly thirty-year career.

Michelle's superior skills, obvious promise, and dedication did not, however, stop the Canadian Forces from firing her. Why? She was gay. Michelle decided to fight the discrimination in Canada's military and its government at a time when being gay was much less accepted than it is today. In fact, being gay was often reviled. Her courageous action opened the doors to improved rights and greater acceptance of gay people. Michelle served the public in a way she never had expected, and became a hero in a way she could never have foreseen.

Michelle was born December 30, 1963, in Ottawa, the capital of Canada. Her mother was a homemaker and her father worked for the government. His thirty-five years in public service helped inspire Michelle's own career aspirations. The family moved to Dartmouth, Nova Scotia, when she was a child, and Michelle and her younger sister spent their childhood there. Eventually, the family moved back to Ontario, where Michelle returned to Ottawa for university. In 1985 she earned a Bachelor of Arts degree, majoring in law.

It wasn't until she finished university that Michelle began to think of the military as a choice for her life's work. At first, she was applying for police jobs. Then she visited the armed forces recruiting center near her family's home. They were eager to have her, and the more she thought about it, the more excited she became. She decided it was the right place for her, and on November 26, 1986, just before her twenty-third birthday, she joined the Canadian Forces. Michelle excelled at her training, and earned the rank of second lieutenant. In 1987, she was sent to Quebec, a French-speaking province, for language education. That is where she fell in love, and the person she loved was a fellow woman officer.

Michelle had not thought of herself as lesbian until this happened. It hadn't even crossed her mind. When she realized she was gay, she wasn't frightened or anxious, as many young people are when they make this discovery. Instead, it just "felt really, really right" and "the natural course" for her to follow. At the same time, she knew the military's punishment for anyone homosexual, male or female, was severe. There was a rule called the Canadian Forces Administrative Order, or CFAO 19-20, that governed what was called "sexual deviation." It said, "Service policy does not allow homosexual members or members with a sexual abnormality to be retained in the Canadian forces." CFAO 19-20 treated homosexuality as a perversion. Michelle knew there were other gay people in the Canadian Forces, but she and they had to be extremely cautious.

With CFAO 19-20, the military was contradicting the law of its own land. Canada abolished laws that made homosexuality a crime in 1969, almost twenty years before Michelle signed up. In addition, in 1985, the year before she joined, Section 15 of the Canadian Charter of Rights and Freedoms came into effect. It guaranteed protection from discrimination to a wide range of groups. The military policy against gays, established in 1967, was also apparently defying Canada's constitution, even though the constitution is regarded as a country's "supreme law."

Why were the armed forces so opposed to gay people? It was all due to prejudice and myth. Michelle says the military leadership was almost entirely male at the time and had "ridiculous and absurd" ideas, especially about gay men. They thought

The words we use

Acceptable words used to describe someone attracted to a person of the same gender have changed over the years. The word homosexual was first used in the 1800s; it's from the Greek word "homos," meaning "same." Some people avoid it, partly because it has been used in negative ways by groups like the military. The words gay and lesbian are often preferred. Gay is used for men, but also for women. Lesbian is used only for women. The term queer used to be an insult, but some people have started using it to describe themselves. Others reject it; they think "queer" suggests they are strange, or deviant. LGBT, which stands for Lesbian, Gay, Bisexual, and Transgender, is used to describe various groups representing these different communities.

gays were uncontrollable deviants, who would sexually attack other soldiers. Military leaders said the troops' unity and morale would be affected if gay people were allowed in. They thought enemy countries would blackmail homosexuals because of their secret lifestyle and turn them into spies or traitors. Michelle points out how ridiculous this was, since it was the military itself that was forcing gays to hide their sexual identities. The military also said allowing gays to serve would mean there would have to be four different sets of bathrooms: two separate ones for heterosexual and homosexual men, and the same for women. This last argument was particularly ridiculed when the policy came under scrutiny.

Decades later, Michelle says she regrets she didn't see that the military was wrong, before it affected her own life. "I wish I didn't have to taste discrimination before I stood up against it." But she didn't want to lose a job she loved and was good at. She hadn't even told her family she was gay; only a few friends knew.

In June 1988, Michelle was given a plum assignment with the Special Investigations Unit (SIU) in Toronto. This unit was part of the Military Police. It investigated suspected cases of spying, as well as criminal activities and cases of suspected homosexuality. Michelle hadn't been in her new job long before the military began investigating her. The woman she was in a relationship with was under military scrutiny, suspected of being gay. Michelle thinks someone reported their relationship, and that's why she, too, became suspect.

In July 1988, just one month after starting her SIU work, her boss told her to get her things together; they had to fly to another city to investigate an important case. She believed they were headed to the airport when the car pulled into a hotel. Her boss then escorted her to a room where two military men waited. They conducted detailed interrogations about her sexuality and sex life for two days, grilling her over and over, trying to get her to say she was gay.

She denied it at first, knowing she could lose her entire career. Later, an organization reviewing Michelle's case blasted the military for "deplorable" conduct and said the officers were wrong to question her about her sexual activities, and to have done it in such an offensive manner.

After the interrogation, Michelle was strapped to a lie detector. But she'd had enough. "Okay, you win," she said, and told them she was indeed lesbian. Then they wanted her to name others she knew in the military who were gay. She absolutely refused. They told her it was obvious she was more loyal to gay people than to her own country, and soon, she would be gone.

Michelle's top-secret security clearance was taken away, and she was transferred to lower-level work. The military also threatened to tell her family she was gay if she didn't, so she was forced to come out to them. She says she can't emphasize enough how supportive they were. Despite the injustice of what had happened, however, Michelle was not considering doing anything about it. Gay rights and being gay were still controversial. The risk of public attention, of people protesting and condemning who she was, frightened her.

The evolution of gay rights

Gay activism did not really become visible until later in the 20th century. Before that, homosexuality was against the law in many countries, with the "crime" punishable by jail sentences. There was also outright hatred of gay people. In Nazi Germany, they were taken to concentration camps and killed, as were other groups the Nazis hated, such as Jews. Britain changed its law against homosexuality in 1967, and Canada did so two years later, but in the U.S. some laws were still on the books until 2003. Gay rights organizations began to grow in the 1970s and '80s. A prominent issue then was the fight against the HIV/AIDS disease that affected gay men. Other issues included a push for laws to stop discrimination in areas such as employment.

Political firsts

Gay people have become more prominent in politics in the 21st century; Americans elected their first openly gay senator in 2012, and Canada's first openly gay provincial premier took office in 2013. The first head of government who was openly gay was the prime minister of Iceland, appointed in 2009. All were women.

Her attitude began to change after a meeting with Canada's first openly gay federal politician, Svend Robinson. Michelle was still in the military when she heard him speak at a gathering in Toronto. Robinson was a Member of Parliament and had recently told the country his sexual orientation. He was a strong promoter of human rights of all kinds and was keen to end the military's discrimination against gays. After his talk, Michelle approached him and briefly told him her story. He followed up later with a phone call. He wanted her to meet Clayton Ruby, a well-known human rights lawyer. Michelle was at "a fork in the road." Should she take legal action against the Canadian Forces? If she did, she might become a target for people who hated gays. She was nervous in the meeting with Ruby, and couldn't decide what to do.

The military, however, had made up its mind about her. In the spring of 1989, they sent her a notification. Although the base commander she worked for raved about her, saying she was one of the best he had ever worked with, praising her "dedication, drive, energy" and initiative, Michelle was told she would be released from the Canadian Forces because "of her admitted homosexual activities contrary to Canadian Forces policy." If she didn't agree to leave, her career would be completely limited by the military's regulations that made her ineligible for promotion, transfer, or further training. She was, in essence, being fired.

In June, Michelle reluctantly signed the release, believing she had no alternative. She was sad and scared, but she was also angry. "I couldn't believe I could be fired on that basis." When she signed the release, she also blasted the Canadian Forces' "true ignorance." She called its policy "archaic, discriminatory, and blatantly unjust."

The next time lawyer Clayton Ruby asked her, "Well, are you going to fight this? Yes or no?" she said yes. Michelle launched her lawsuit against the Canadian Forces for $550,000 in January, 1990, on the grounds that her human rights had been violated under the Charter of Rights and Freedoms. Still frightened about going public, she asked Ruby if they could take legal action without using her name. Of course, they couldn't. But to this day she appreciates that some people were sensitive to her fear. One well-known newspaper columnist, Michele Landsberg, willingly disguised Michelle's identity in one of the first pieces written about her case. Landsberg's column took the military to task for its treatment of this "shining star of the Armed Forces," saying they had lost an outstanding officer, and calling the Forces' intolerance of homosexuals "ridiculous."

Landsberg was among the first to publicly berate the Canadian Forces for its policy, and what it did to Michelle, but she was not the last. Still, over the next two years, the military refused to budge. Besides her court action, Michelle appealed to a government body called the Security Intelligence Review Committee to reverse the decision to remove her top security clearance.

In August 1990, SIRC's report said the military and the government should give Michelle back her job, and her top security clearance. The committee was outraged at what had happened to Michelle and said the military's policy against gays was contrary to the country's Charter of Rights and Freedoms.

It seemed like a victory. Then, the government and military decided to appeal the ruling, and everything was put on hold.

The *Toronto Star* newspaper, responding to the SIRC decision, called the military's policy against gays "madness," and said it "was time to commit the armed forces to true equality" and assign the "policy of bigotry to the trash bin where it belongs."

For a brief period in 1991, it actually looked like that might happen. Headlines in newspapers across the country that October declared the government would announce a policy change any day. The government even notified U.S. military leaders in the Pentagon that it was about to drop its ban on gays. Public opinion polls on gays in the military showed a majority of Canadians supported the move. The government, however, took a sudden step backwards. Some politicians in the ruling Progressive Conservative government rebelled, and the new policy was put on the shelf.

Tuesday, October 27, 1992, was to be Michelle's day in court. It had been more than three years since she had been released from the Forces, and more than two years since she had launched her legal suit. Despite public opinion, the law of the land, and the rulings of government bodies, the military had changed nothing about its policy on gays. The trial case – "Douglas versus Canada" – was about to begin. Michelle told the media that she was glad the long wait was over, and that she was not doing this just for herself. "It's for the people who are still in the Canadian Armed Forces and for those who never had the chance to take this to court. There's no question there are people still being harmed by this policy...." She meant all those still in the military who were hiding their sexual orientation to keep their jobs.

On the court day, the Defence Department and the Canadian Forces finally and suddenly surrendered. They agreed to an order from a Federal Court judge that the anti-gay policy be dropped, because it violated the Charter of Rights and Freedoms. They could no longer ignore the constitution and make up their own law on this matter. Michelle was "jubilant," and both she and her lawyer celebrated the fact that her case would help gay people from that day forward. "Today is one thing," Michelle said, "but for evermore they will be equal members. It's something I fought for a long time."

She also received $100,000 as part of the decision. Other lawsuits by other Forces members whose careers were damaged by the policy were quietly settled in the months following Michelle's case. And despite her fears about going public, she did not receive one piece of negative mail through her entire legal proceedings.

Decades later, Michelle lives in Ottawa, with her partner, and works for the federal government's Department of Justice. She volunteered an enormous number of hours as the founding President of the Foundation for Equal Families, which dealt with challenges to same-sex relationships and gay rights, and she now serves as Chair of the Board for Free the Children Canada. She doesn't lament the opportunities she missed because she was forced to give up her military career.

The changing United States

Before 1993, the United States banned gay people. Then the ban was changed somewhat; service personnel were banned from being *openly* gay. The policy was dubbed "Don't Ask, Don't Tell," because if gays and lesbians were open about their sexuality, they could be thrown out of the military. Some reports say this happened to more than 12,500 people during the policy's eighteen years. In Canada's much smaller military, a study showed that in a six-year period before Michelle Douglas' case, between 1986 and 1992, sixty people were discharged for homosexuality, and another fifteen were denied promotions. "Don't Ask, Don't Tell" ended in September, 2011. U.S. President Barack Obama welcomed the end of the American policy he said forced people to "lie about who they are."

In fact, she says, she is grateful because it "changed my life for the better." She believes what she has done is more meaningful than anything she would have achieved otherwise. Intolerance of gays was "un-Canadian," and she sees the challenges and the risks she took as a patriotic act that helped make Canada a better country.

SHANNEN KOOSTACHIN

"... NEVER give up hope. Get up, pick up your books, and GO TO SCHOOL."

1994 – 2010

Shannen Koostachin was thirteen years old when she met Chuck Strahl in his posh government offices in Canada's capital city of Ottawa in May of 2008. He was tall, and a cabinet minister, one of the most powerful politicians ruling the country. But Shannen wasn't shy or afraid, and she didn't care how imposing Strahl was. She had travelled more than 600 miles (965 kilometers) from her remote northern community for one purpose: to persuade the minister to change his mind. For eight years the government had been promising to give Shannen's community a decent school for its children. Recently, Strahl had cancelled that promise.

Shannen began her conversation by telling the minister she wished she and her brothers and sisters had a school to go to that looked as nice as his offices. But then Strahl told Shannen and the others with her he was standing firm: there would be no new school for Attawapiskat First Nation. Shannen stood her ground as well. She shook Strahl's hand and told him, "We're not going to quit."

Shannen Koostachin was at the forefront of what would come to be called the biggest youth-led children's rights campaign in Canadian history. She became the face of a movement bent on obtaining a basic right for her people: a good education.

Across the country, other school children rallied behind her and her schoolmates. She spoke to media at news conferences, to school boards, teachers, students, religious groups, and workers' organizations. She was nominated for the International Children's Peace Prize, awarded to children whose courageous actions make a difference for children around the world.

Anyone who saw her speak, live or on video, was astounded by this young teenager's passion and strength. She was so effective and powerful in all she did that Shannen's campaign for a school was able to continue even after her death. Almost two years to the day that she met the cabinet minister, on May 31, 2010, she was killed in a car accident. While her family, friends, and community mourned, and newspapers reported the loss of a fifteen-year-old who had a national impact, Shannen's Dream was founded to continue her fight for equality.

Shannen Noella Jane Koostachin was born July 12, 1994, on an isolated reserve on the coast of James Bay in northern Ontario. Attawapiskat First Nation is a community of nearly 2,000 people. The nearest urban center is about 300 miles (485 kilometers) south. It's not even possible to drive to Attawapiskat; you have to fly in. In English, her tribal group and the first language she spoke are called Cree, but Shannen used the Aboriginal name, Mushkegowuk Innanu. Her parents were Jenny and Andrew Koostachin, and she had three brothers and three sisters.

Attawapiskat did have an elementary school when Shannen was a little girl. Built in 1976 by the Canadian government, it was the kind of school Shannen would later demand they have again – "comfy," sturdy, and modern. It was also on land where diesel fuel, used for heating, was stored underground. Unknown to the community, thousands of gallons of the fuel leaked into the soil causing a terrible smell that nauseated students and teachers, and gave them headaches. Parents could smell fumes on their children when they returned from school.

Shannen Koostachin

Throughout the 1980s and '90s, the problem was investigated, and a partial cleanup was done. But in 2000, when a report said the chemical contamination in the school area was unacceptable for human health, parents demanded action.

The chief and council and education authorities closed the school permanently and eventually it was torn down. Portables were installed for the classes up to Grade 8. They were intended as a temporary solution because a new school was supposedly in the works. But this was the beginning of a trail of broken government promises.

The portables had many problems. They let in -20 degree winter air through leaky doors and windows, and had holes where mice came in. Children and teachers had to go outside many times throughout the day, moving from building to building, in weather that includes blizzards and ice storms. The bathroom was right in the classroom, and students felt embarrassed to use it with others sitting right outside the door. There was no library, art or music room, and the classrooms were small. Many children in Attawapiskat, discouraged by the conditions, simply stopped attending school. The reserve's education director said 15 percent left before Grade 8.

Shannen's campaign brought attention to the inequalities in education that Aboriginal children face across Canada. According to some reports, $2,000 less per year is spent on education for each Aboriginal student, than is spent on other Canadian children. The national government is responsible for Aboriginal schooling, and it doesn't provide money for libraries, computers, science labs, and many other facilities that most children, and their parents, expect. First Nations people have some control of their children's education, such as deciding what they will study. But the government in Ottawa had the authority to decide whether or not Attawapiskat got a new school.

Less than the rest

The difference in funds for Aboriginal education is partly due to an age-old split in government responsibilities. The public education of all children, except Aboriginals, is paid for by Canada's provinces. The federal government pays for Aboriginal education, but it spends up to 25 percent less for primary school children on First Nations reserves than the provincial governments pay for other children. One Canadian magazine called Aboriginal students "an education underclass." A respected economist wrote their education situation was "a failure," and he only had one explanation for why Aboriginal students got less: "we don't care enough."

Between 2000 and 2007, three different cabinet ministers for the Aboriginal Affairs department promised there would be money for a school. But nothing happened. Then in December, 2007, after Chuck Strahl was appointed as minister, the community learned it would be at least five years before there would be funds to build a new school. It got worse. Three months after that, the minister said other Aboriginal communities were a higher priority than Attawapiskat, and he couldn't say exactly when a school might be built.

Shannen and many other students were fed up. They had spent their entire school life in portables. No more waiting – it was time to take action. Charlie Angus, the politician representing Attawapiskat, was a member of the New Democratic Party that opposed the ruling Conservative Party. He met with the students and told them he could help them run a campaign that would draw attention to their plight and perhaps force the government to change its mind.

And so the battle began, one that would eventually include thousands of other school children across Canada. Angus posted a video on YouTube, showing the conditions in Attawapiskat's portables. He publicly challenged Strahl in the House of Commons, where elected Members of Parliament meet to argue national affairs. He asked why Attawapiskat First Nation should have to put up with the government's neglect. The minister denied any wrongdoing and said the portables posed no health concerns. Nearly 60,000 people watched Angus's video, and students across Canada began a letter-writing campaign to support the Attawapiskat students. The story of the portables, and the government's refusal to do anything, began to make the news. Shannen created her own YouTube video. In it she pleaded, "Please don't ignore us just because we're different...Please don't forget us...We've been waiting for a school for too long."

By March 2008, Ontario's public school boards, responsible for more than two million students, were encouraging students to write protest letters to the minister. One board representative explained why. "All children have the right to a quality education," she said, "and we want the students of Attawapiskat to know their peers care about them." The minister's office was flooded with letters.

The Grade 8 Attawapiskat students then made an important decision. Like many graduating classes, they were planning a trip near the end of the school year, and had decided to visit Niagara Falls, in southern Ontario. But May 29th was the date set for a National Aboriginal Day of Action – a day of demonstrations across the country to draw attention to problems faced by Canadian First Nations. What better day to bring attention to Attawapiskat's need for a school, and the government's broken promises? Shannen's class decided to give up the fun trip they had planned in exchange for something more meaningful. Twenty-one Grade 8 students would make the long journey to

The Day of Action march to Parliament Hill

the nation's capital and join the protest. Some students from Southern Ontario who had written letters to the government about Attawapiskat decided they would go as well.

Shannen and her classmates began their protest action in Ottawa with a news conference on May 28. Flanked by two classmates, Shannen spoke coolly and calmly into the microphones. She told the reporters it was not the first time a teenager from Attawapiskat had been to Ottawa to publicize the need for a school. Three years earlier her older sister Serena had also gone to the capital to speak with the media and meet with a cabinet minister. That was 2005, and that minister had promised Attawapiskat a school. Shannen asked, "Why do I have to come back and do the same thing once again? As young people we are told to keep our promises. But our own government cannot keep a promise that they have made three times."

The reporters wrote articles about the students, and spoke to Attawapiskat teachers as well. One said she had taught at a school on a poor island in the Pacific Ocean before going to Attawapiskat. She said she was shocked to see many of the same conditions in the reserve's school. "I couldn't even believe I was in my own province." The First Nations chief who spoke for all Aboriginal people in Canada said he wondered if the government's response would be different "if this was a situation in Toronto, Ottawa (or) any urban community in the country."

The next day, May 29th, was the Day of Action. Students from Attawapiskat, joined by their supporters, led hundreds of people in the protest march to Parliament Hill, the site of Canada's government. They carried signs reading, "Education is a Right." It was the face-to-face meeting with Strahl, however, that was to be the most important moment for Shannen and the students and tribal elders with her.

Their excitement and hopes were quickly dashed. Once again, the minister said no. No new school, because other

Shannen speaks to the crowd at the Day of Action.

communities needed schools more than they did. No, because Ottawa had spent $5 million on the portables and on the nearby high school, so elementary students could use its gym. Strahl also said Attawapiskat's leaders were given money each year to make necessary repairs, and maintenance of the buildings was their responsibility.

The minister's face-to-face "no" seemed to put even greater steel into Shannen's spine and spirit.

After telling Strahl they wouldn't quit, she went outside and told the crowd of about 1,000 on Parliament Hill what had happened. They responded with cries of "Shame!" She told reporters that after Strahl said no, "I cried and some of my friends cried and some of my elders cried." Newspapers wrote of the teen's "poise beyond her years." Charlie Angus was appalled. "If there's one thing that we can put money into, it has to be the education of children," he said.

The only good news was the attention the students received, especially Shannen. It meant more people were learning about their cause, and momentum against the government began to grow. Angus says

"These children . . . "

The Assembly of First Nations is an organization of Aboriginal leaders in Canada, and the National Chief represents them all. Phil Fontaine was National Chief at the time Attawapiskat students were organizing their protest. He told them he was proud they were speaking out. After their disappointing meeting with Strahl, Fontaine said the minister was right in one respect: there were horrible conditions in other First Nations schools, and 39 First Nations communities had no school of any kind. But he said that meant the government needed to make First Nations children a priority, fix all the schools, and give Attawapiskat children what they asked for. "These children are being short-changed," he said, "and it can't be allowed to continue."

Shannen didn't want to be an activist, or a leader, but she was a spirited young woman who couldn't tolerate the hopelessness of young children on her reserve, and she believed in standing up and fighting for her community. She also had an uncanny ability to capture an audience and make news headlines. He said this was astounding given that her first language was Cree, and she had grown up in such an isolated place.

In the summer of 2008, just after Shannen's fourteenth birthday, she and a team of Attawapiskat students took their protest to an international level. They informed the federal government they were going to ask the United Nations to investigate their case. The UN is the world's premier organization of countries, and its missions include monitoring the treatment of children and children's rights. The Attawapiskat students would ask the UN if Canada was meeting its obligations according to UN requirements for the care and protection of children.

The autumn brought an unwelcome change for Shannen. Her parents decided she should go to high school in New Liskeard, Ontario, which was off the reserve. Angus said it

An international impact

Shannen was encouraged to write the UN by Cindy Blackstock, who had heard her speak in Ottawa. Blackstock has been a committed activist for First Nations children for more then twenty years and was also the person who put Shannen's name forward for the International Children's Peace Prize. She is just one of many Canadian Aboriginal women activists who have had a national and international impact. Mary Two-Axe Earley lobbied the Canadian government for years over discrimination against Aboriginal women in Canadian law. Sandra Lovelace Nicholas went to the UN in 1977 to protest the same issue. She won her case at the UN, and a Royal Commission agreed with Two-Axe Earley, but it took years for the Canadian government to make the legal change.

broke Shannen's heart to leave her home, but she wanted to become a lawyer, and this was the best decision for her education and future. Still, Shannen continued her activities on behalf of Attawapiskat. In November, she spoke at a forum in Toronto attended by hundreds of students, as well as teachers and school board representatives. Shannen told them, "When you know other children have big comfy schools with hallways that are warm, you feel like you don't count for anything." Students who heard her were outraged at the unfairness. The following year, 2009, she was the keynote speaker at the Ontario Federation of Labour's convention; the OFL represents one million workers and has a strong political voice. Then, in December, there was a surprise announcement. Chuck Strahl, speaking to First Nations chiefs, said negotiations would begin to build a school in Attawapiskat. Shannen and the other children of Attawapiskat, and all those children and adults who supported them, had won.

On the evening of May 31 the following year, Shannen was returning from a holiday with family friend Rose Thornton, 56, and two other friends. Their minivan collided with a truck, and Shannen and Thornton were killed. There was an outpouring of tributes to Shannen from all those who knew her or knew of her because of her actions on behalf of her people. Shannen's Dream was founded to carry forward her goal of equality in education for Aboriginal children. Its victories include getting a bill passed in the House of Commons in February, 2012, that said the Canadian government would adopt Shannen's Dream by declaring all First Nations children have an equal right to high-quality education and by committing the necessary finances to make this so. The government agreed to invest about $90 million a year, for three years, to improve Aboriginal education. But critics say the funding for First Nation schools is still too low, and that September, the UN took Canada to task for not meeting its standards with respect

Half a world away

The case of another young girl who fought for education rights half a world away from Shannen's country made international headlines in 2012. Malala Yousafzai was fourteen years old when she was shot in the head and neck in October that year by a Taliban gunman while she was riding a school bus in Pakistan. She was a known campaigner for the rights of girls to attend school. The Taliban, an extreme Islamist group, does not believe girls should be educated. She survived, but was flown to a British hospital for surgeries. Malala remained defiant and said she would keep up her campaign for girls' rights to go to school.

to the care and protection of children. It said Canada needed to greatly improve what it did for Aboriginals, especially since it is one of the top five economies in the world. And by 2012, three years after Strahl's promise, the school in Attawapiskat still hadn't been built. Construction had started, however, and reports said the $31 million facility was expected to open in 2013.

After her death, many people tried to explain what it was about Shannen that made her such an inspiring leader at such a young age. But Shannen spoke for herself. In a letter she wrote as part of her nomination for the International Children's Peace Prize, she said she had always been taught to look up to the Seven Grandfathers: Love, Respect, Truth, Honesty, Humility, Bravery, and Wisdom. She said her father also taught her to take three steps in life: "putting God first, then family, and then education." She wanted people to know she didn't like broken promises. And finally, writing about what she would do to inspire others, she said, "I would tell them NEVER give up hope. Get up, pick up your books, and GO TO SCHOOL. But not in portables."

SOURCES AND RESOURCES

Olympe de Gouges

Beckstrand,Lisa. *Deviant Women of the French Revolution and the Rise of Feminism.* N.J. Associated University Press, 2009

Cole, John R. *Between the Queen and the Cabby.* McGill-Queen's University Press, 2011

De Mattos, Rudy Frédéric. *The Discourse of Women Writers in the French Revolution: Olympe de Gouges and Constance de Salm.* The University of Texas at Austin, 2007

Moore, Lucy. *Liberty; The Lives of Six Women in Revolutionary France.* Harper Press, 2006

Mousset, Sophie. *Women's Rights and the French Revolution.* Transaction Publishers, 2007

The website *Liberty, Equality, Fraternity; Exploring the French Revolution* has good summaries of this period of history:
http://chnm.gmu.edu/revolution/

Sojouner Truth

Clift, Eleanor. *Founding Sisters and the Nineteenth Amendment.* New Jersey. John Wiley & Sons Inc., 2003

Haywood, Chanta M. *Prophesying Daughters: Black Women Preachers and the Word, 1823-1913.* University of Missouri, 2003

Mabee, Carleton and Newhouse, Susan Mabee. *Sojourner Truth: Slave, Prophet, Legend.* New York. New York University Press,1993

Painter, Nell Irvin. *Sojourner Truth; A Life, A Symbol.* W.W. Norton & Company, New York, NY 1996

Stetson, Erlene and David, Linda. *Glorying in Tribulation; The Lifework of Sojourner Truth.* Michigan State University Press, East Lansing, 1994

Truth, Sojourner. *Narrative of Sojourner Truth.* Vintage Classics,1993

Washington,Margaret. *Sojourner Truth's America.* University of Illinois Press, Urbana and Chicago, 2009

Whalin, W. Terry. *Sojourner Truth: American Abolitionist.* Chelsea House Publishers U.S., 1999

Sarojini Naidu

Agrawal, Lion M.G. *Freedom Fighters of India.* Isha Books, Delhi, India, 2008

Banerjee, Hasi. *Sarojini Naidu, the traditional feminist.* Monograph, Univ. of Calcutta, 1998

Louis, Wm. Roger (editor). *Adventures with Brittania.* First University of Texas Press, 1996

Naidu, Sarojini. *Speeches and Writings of Sarojini Naidu.* Madras G.A. Natesan and Co., 1925

Naravane, Vishwanath. *Sarojini Naidu; An Introduction to Her Life, Work and Poetry.* Orient Longman, Hyderabad, India, 1980

Nolen, Stephanie. "Caste: A Turbulent History." *The Globe and Mail,* June, 2012

The Mahatma and the Poetess; Selection of letters between Gandhiji and Sarojini Naidu. Compiled by E.S. Reddy, edited by Mrinalini Sarabhai. Bhartiya Vidya Bhavan. 1998

Sengupta, P.S. *Sarojini Naidu: A Biography.* Asia Publishing House, London, 1966

There are a number of good online articles about the history of the Salt March of 1930.They include *Women in the Indian Independence Movement,* from the University of Texas at Austin

Ruth First

First, Ruth. *117 Days: An Account of Confinement and Interrogation Under the South African 90-Day Detention Law.* London. Bloomsbury, 1988

Frankel, Glenn. "South Africa's White Communist; Joe Slovo Wants to End Apartheid With a Gun." *The Washington Post.* July 14, 1985

Frankel, Glenn. *Rivonia's Children: Three Families and the Cost of Conscience in White South Africa.* New York. Farrar, Straus and Giroux, 1999

Mandela, Nelson. *No Easy Walk to Freedom.* London. Heinemann, 1965

Pinnock, Don. *Voices of Liberation, Volume Two, Ruth First* Pretoria. HSRC Publishers, 1997

Seligman, David. "Facing the Evil." *The Jerusalem Report,* Feb. 28, 2000

Slovo, Gillian. *Every Secret Thing: My Family, My Country.* Little, Brown, 1998

Gloria Steinem
Hass, Nancy. "Gloria Steinem Still Wants More." *Newsweek,* Aug. 15, 2011

Heilbrun, Carolyn G. *Education of a Woman: The Life of Gloria Steinem.* New York. Ballantine Books, 1995.

Hepola, Sarah. "A Woman Like No Other." *The New York Times,* March 18, 2012

Kurlansky, Mark. *1968: The Year that Rocked the World.* New York. Random House, 2004

Maclean's. "A Close Watch on Feminism." Nov. 16, 1987

Pogrebin, Abigail. "How Do You Spell Ms.?" *New York Magazine,* Nov. 7, 2011

Steinem, Gloria. "After Black Power, Women's Liberation." *New York Magazine,* April 4, 1969

Steinem, Gloria. "Women's Liberation Aims to Free Men Too." *The Washington Post,* June 7, 1970

Steinem, Gloria. *Outrageous Acts and Everyday Rebellions. Second Edition.* New York. Henry Holt and Company, 1995

Steinem, Gloria. "The Accidental Activist." ABC-TV interview, 2003

Stern, Sydney Ladensohn. *Gloria Steinem: Her Passions, Politics and Mystique.* Birch Lane Press, 1998

Weller, Sheila. "The Woman Who Started It All." *Glamour,* December, 2011

Joan Baez

Baez, Joan. *And A Voice to Sing With: A Memoir*. New York. Summit Books, 1987

Chambers, John Whiteclay. *The Oxford Companion to American Military History*. Oxford University Press, 2000

Evans, Mike and Kingsbury, Paul. *Woodstock: Three Days that Rocked the World*. Sterling Publishing Company, Inc., 2009

Grunwald, Lisa and Adler, Stephen J. *Women's Letters: America from the Revolutionary War to the Present*. Random House Digital Inc., 2009

Hajdu, David. *Positively 4th Street: The Life and Times of Joan Baez, Bob Dylan, Mimi Baez Farina and Richard Farina*. Picador, 2011

Moss, Mary. "Joanie wasn't Phoanie": Joan Baez and the Vietnam Anti-War Movement." *The Banyan Quarterly*. Vol. 1 No. I, Winter 2000

Spector, Mark and Wharton, Mary, producers. *Joan Baez: How Sweet the Sound*. American Masters Series. PBS, 2009

Time Magazine. "Sibyl with Guitar." Nov. 23, 1962

Joan Baez' own website: http://www.joanbaez.com

Thomas Merton Award website: http://www.thomasmertoncenter.org

Leilani Muir

Goyette, Linda. "Sterilization Victim Deserves Every Penny." *Calgary Herald,* Jan. 27, 1996

Gunter, Lorne. "Playing God is man's folly; Left and right have wrongly promoted eugenics." *Edmonton Journal,* Sept. 23, 1997

Muir V. Alberta. Alberta Court of Queen's Bench, Veit J. Jan. 25, 1996

Nemeth, Mary and Johnson, Bart. "Nobody has the Right to Play God." *Maclean's,* June 26, 1995

Thomas, Don. "Proposed settlement leaves woman angry." *Calgary Herald,* Dec. 15, 1995

"Sterilized woman gets $750,000." *Calgary Herald,* Jan. 26, 1996

Tremonti, Anna Maria. Interview with Leilani Muir. *The Current,* CBC-Radio, Nov. 14, 2011

Wahlsten, Douglas. *Leilani Muir versus the philosopher king: Eugenics on trial in Alberta.* Genetica, 1997

Whiting, Glynis. Director. *The Sterilization of Leilani Muir.* National Film Board of Canada, 1996

Temple Grandin

Cutler, Eustacia. *A Thorn in My Pocket: Temple Grandin's mother tells the family story.* Future Horizons, 2004

Friend, Catherine. *The Compassionate Carnivore.* De Capo Press, 2009

Glaister, Dan. "Drawing on autistic licence." *The Guardian* (London), June 2, 2005

Grandin, Temple. *Emergence Labelled Autistic.* Costello,1986

Grandin, Temple. *Thinking in Pictures: and other reports from my life with autism.* Vintage Books, 1996

Grandin, Temple and Johnson, Catherine. *Animals in Translation: using the mysteries of autism to decode animal behaviour.* Simon and Schuster, 2009

Grandin, Temple. Websites: http://www.grandin.com and http://www.templegrandin.com

Montgomery, Sy. *Temple Grandin: How the girl who loved cows embraced autism and changed the world.* Houghton Mifflin Books for Children, 2012

Sacks, Oliver. *An Anthropologist on Mars: seven paradoxical tales.* Vintage Books, 1995

Specter, Michael. "The Extremist; The woman behind the most successful radical group in America." *The New Yorker,* April 14, 2003

Michelle Douglas

Belkin, Aaron and McNichol, Jason. "Homosexual personnel policy in the Canadian Forces." *International Journal,* Winter 2000-2001

Bindman, Stephen. "Military admits policy wrong; agrees to welcome gays, lesbians." *The Ottawa Citizen,* Oct. 28, 1992

Crysdale, Joy. Interviews with Michelle Douglas. 2012

Douglas, Michelle V. Her Majesty the Queen. Trial Division, Mackay J. Toronto Oct. 27, 1992; Ottawa Dec. 1, 1992

Landsberg, Michele. "This is military intelligence?" *Toronto Star,* Mar. 31, 1990

Martz, Ron. "Gays in the Military." *The Atlanta Journal and Constitution,* Jan. 29, 1993.

Sherman, Geraldine. "Truth and Consequences." *Toronto Life,* May 2004

Toronto Star. "A case of homophobia." Editorial, Oct. 15, 1991.

Website on terms: LGBT Terms and Definitions. International + LGBT at the University of Michigan.
http://internationalspectrum.umich.edu/life/definitions

Shannen Koostachin

Angus, Charlie. "A Tribute to Shannen Koostachin." Provincial Advocate for Children and Youth in Ontario, *provincialadvocate. on.ca/documents/en/Shannen.pdf*

Bailey, Sue. "Native children fight for school." *The Daily Gleaner* (New Brunswick), May 30, 2008

Brown, Louise. "School boards join reserve fight." *Toronto Star,* March 14, 2008

"Reserve teens want school building." *Toronto Star,* Nov. 27, 2008

Curry, Bill. "Native pupils ask Strahl for school; But minister rejects plea for new building." *The Globe and Mail,* May 30, 2008

Diebel, Linda. "Native students go away disappointed." *Toronto Star,* May 30, 2008

German, Amy. "In memory of Shannen Noella Jane Koostachin." *nationnews.ca,* June 18, 2010

Godbout, Arielle. "Northern students lobby for long-promised school." *Ottawa Citizen,* May 29, 2008

Goyette, Linda. "Still Waiting in Attawapiskat." *Canadian Geographic,* Dec. 2010

Koostachin, Shannen. "Students of Attawapiskat Plead to Minister Chuck Strahl." Youtube, March, 2008

Meili, Dianne. "Shannen Koostachin – youth leader led the fight for new school and children's rights." *Windspeaker,* Vol. 28 Issue 5, 2010

Sniderman, Andrew Stobo. "Aboriginal students: an education underclass." *Maclean's,* Aug. 8, 2012

Wilson, Janet. *Shannen and the Dream for a School.* Toronto. Second Story Press, 2011

ACKNOWLEDGMENTS

Researching and writing this book I had the opportunity to learn about the lives of many brave, idealistic and dedicated women, and there can't be anything much better than that. My thanks to publisher Margie Wolfe for offering me the privilege of writing for the Women's Hall of Fame series a second time. Thank you to all the fabulous women at Second Story. Managing editor Carolyn Jackson's support was kind, generous, and calming, and Melissa Kaita's design work was, as always, wonderful. Intern and fact-checker Amanda Thomas saved the day more than once with her research. Editor Kathryn White's editing, encouragement, and feedback made for vast improvements. April Lindgren generously contributed her considerable professional talent and expert eyes to the final product.

I would not have been able to do this book without the generous support and backing of people at Humber College. Thank you especially to former dean of the School of Media Studies William Hanna and to Vice President Academic Michael Hatton and Vice President Human Resources Deb McCarthy. Thank you also to Associate Dean Basil Guinane for his leadership and guidance.

Determining exactly who to include in a collection like this is truly a challenging task, and I owe thanks to the following people who suggested or introduced me to the following women: Rev. Hugh D. Reid for Sojourner Truth, Myra Novogrodsky for Leilani Muir, Michael Enright for Temple Grandin, and for leading me to Shannen Koostachin, who was also suggested by Siobhan Moore. April Lindgren suggested and introduced me to Michelle Douglas. I would also like to thank Michelle for trusting me with her story. I have many debts of gratitude to Karen Levine, who has introduced me to so many great people over the years, and who told me the story of Ruth First years ago.

The Ontario Arts Council has my great appreciation for its work on behalf of writers, including me.

I want to thank my family; brother John Crysdale and his wife Marj, my niece Janina Ganton and her husband Dave, and niece Alycia Crysdale for all they have done and are to me. Finally, I would like to thank Ken Dafoe who always listened, always understood, and always had faith that I could do it. Again, I have to say, there isn't anything much better than that.

PHOTO CREDITS

page 79: © Bill Cotton / Colorado State University

page 89: Steve Jurvetson / Creative Commons

page 91: © Canadian Lesbian and Gay Archives

page 101: © Janet Wilson

page 103: © Janet Wilson

page 106: © Janet Wilson

page 108: © Janet Wilson